RICHARD STRAUSS

RICHARD STRAUSS

BY ERNEST NEWMAN
WITH A PERSONAL
NOTE BY ALFRED KALISCH

GREENWOOD PRESS, PUBLISHERS
WESTPORT, CONNECTICUT

Originally published in 1908
by John Lane: The Bodley Head, London

First Greenwood Reprinting 1970

Library of Congress Catalogue Card Number 79-109806

SBN 8371-4297-0

Printed in the United States of America

PREFACE

I REGRET that I am unable to give to this volume the personal touch that is one of the objects of the series in which it appears. As I have not the honour of Dr. Strauss's acquaintance, I am almost wholly ignorant of his private personality and the details of his daily life ; beyond the fact that he writes his music on ruled paper I can give none of those glimpses into the interior that are so fascinating to all students of great men's lives and works. On the other hand, the absence of even the slightest acquaintance with the subject of the book is not without its compensations, in that it makes a more independent critical attitude possible to the writer. Some interesting particulars of Richard Strauss the man will be found in the Introduction, which my friend Mr. Kalisch has been kind enough to contribute to the volume.

No one can be more conscious than myself
of the many things that have been left unsaid
in this little book, the many interesting points
in Strauss's work that have not been dwelt
upon. I can only plead that the subject is an
enormous one and the book a very small one.
And as the space at my disposal was so limited,
I thought it better to confine myself to the
broader aspects of Strauss's works—not to
attempt to describe any of them in detail
(beyond telling briefly the stories of the operas),
but to trace the main lines of his intellectual
and musical development, and to indicate
some of the new æsthetic problems that are
raised by his work. " Guides " in plenty can
be had to the larger works themselves. In
English, the best of these are the analyses by
Mr. Kalisch and Mr. Pitt in the Queen's Hall
programme books. Still more copious analyses
are to be had in German, in the excellent
series of " Musikführer " and " Opernführer,"
published by Messrs. Seemann of Leipzig.
Students who wish to pursue further the
critical study of Strauss may turn to Gustav
Brecher's " Richard Strauss, eine mono-
graphische Skizze," Erich Urban's " Richard

Strauss " (in the series of " Moderne Essays
zur Kunst und Litteratur "), the same writer's
lively booklet, " Strauss contra Wagner," the
" Richard Strauss, eine Charakterskizze " of
Arthur Seidl and Wilhelm Klatte, Seidl's
" Der moderne Geist in der deutschen Tonkunst," Hans Merian's booklet on *Also sprach
Zarathustra*, Eugen Schmitz's " Richard Strauss
als Musikdramatiker," the article on Strauss
in Mr. James Huneker's " Overtones," and
the journals of the civilized world, *passim.*
There are at least three admirable books
dealing with *Salome*, each of them with special
excellencies of its own—Mr. Lawrence Gilman's
(John Lane, London), Maurice Kufferath's
(Fischbacher, Paris), and Otto Taubmann's
(Fürstner, Berlin).

E. N.

RICHARD STRAUSS: THE MAN

LIKE all dominant personalities, Strauss possesses in a marked degree the gift of inspiring strong admiration and creating for himself enthusiastic apostles. That he is sometimes not overpleased at their missionary zeal is shown by the story told (with what truth it is impossible to discover) of his remark to a very insistent admirer, who said : " Master, you are the Buddha of modern music," and to whom he answered : " I do not know about that ; but I do know what is the pest." It is, of course, part and parcel of his modernity— an objectionable word, but nothing else expresses the idea so well—that he should have a complex mind and be prone to introspection ; if he had not been born with it, his training and his surroundings would have created it. But there is a point at which he grows impatient of self-analysis, and at bottom there are in him the simplicity and directness which must be the mainspring of all considerable creative activities in all branches of human endeavour.

He was once asked what were the tendencies of modern music, and whither he thought his own music was leading him; and his only answer was : "Ask the writers on music—not the writers of music." This answer is instructive, and has a distinct bearing on his whole artistic creed. It means, of course—unless it is a mere heedless epigram, which is not probable—that he recognizes that there is at the root of all musical inspiration something unconscious which the creative artist himself cannot account for ; and in so far it involves a refutation of those who argue that the doctrine of programme music is incompatible with the presence of any superhuman spiritual element in the art. It is in seeming, but only seeming, contradiction to the well-known saying attributed to him : "There is no such thing as Abstract Music ; there is good music and bad music. If it is good, it means something ; and then it is Programme Music." The best exposition of his artistic creed is that contained in his preface

to the series of booklets on music published by
Bard, Marquardt, and Co., to which reference
is made elsewhere ; but it contains nothing
new for those who have conversed with him
on such topics.

One of the cardinal dogmas in his musical
faith is his love of Mozart, whom he claims as
a " modern " in the sense that his music expresses ideas which appeal to men of this day
more than Beethoven's work. His interpreta-
tions of Mozart are criticized in some quarters
as being too modern, because they impart into
his compositions these very ideas ; but this is
not the place to discuss the justice of such
strictures. It is more to the point to protest that
it is unjust to say, as is so often said, that his
love for Mozart is a mere pose. Any one who
has been in his society during a good performance of a Mozartian masterpiece can vouch for
the sincerity of his worship, at any rate. The
writer remembers his saying once, after he had
heard the Jupiter Symphony with rapt attention : " We can still all of us learn something
from that." In keeping with this is his advice,
habitually given to all very young aspirants
who come to him with portentous Symphonic

b

Poems and tell him that *Tod und Verklärung*
and the *Symphonia Domestica* have been their
models : " Go home and study Haydn's Symphonies and then the Symphonies of Mozart,
and come to me again in two years' time."

Like all great innovators, he has thoroughly
mastered the work of his predecessors, and
there is no doubt that he could write a " cor-
rect " and learned fugue as well as any professor if he wanted to ; that is to say, if it
should ever happen that a fugue should be the
best means of expressing what he had to say.
The score of *Also sprach Zarathustra* is sufficient proof, if proof is needed. In a discussion
on form he once said—or quoted with approval
the saying—that till the time of Liszt and
Wagner the utmost that was permitted to a
composer was to ask himself : " How much
expression can I put into this or that form ? "
whereas the modern composer says to himself :
" How can I modify the form so as to make
it the best possible way of expressing all I
want ? "

This is perhaps the place to mention two
little incidents which show his attitude towards
the unconscious reminiscences in his works.

After the first performance of the *Domestic Symphony* in London some friends pointed out to him that a passage at the beginning of the Nocturne was identical with the beginning of the well-known Gondoliers' song in the first book of Mendelssohn's "Songs without Words." Those who were present at the conversation could have no doubt that the discovery was a complete surprise to him. Similarly he was quite taken aback when at one of the orchestral rehearsals of *Salome* at Dresden a member of the band (who was an Austrian) pointed out to him that one of the love-motifs is one of the cavalry calls in the Austrian army, which he must have heard hundreds of times. One may compare with this the anecdote of Wagner, who, when he was rehearsing *Die Meistersinger*, and came to the passage in the third act when Sachs says to Walther: "Mein Freund, in holder Jugendzeit," remarked, "My friends, this is certainly Nicolai, but I never knew it till to-day," meaning that the phrase is identical with the principal melody of the overture to *The Merry Wives of Windsor*, with which he must have been perfectly familiar when he wrote it.

In his work Strauss is fastidiously methodi-

cal, and his writing-table is a model of neat-
ness which would put to shame the most
precise of business men. All his manuscripts
and his sketch books are arranged, indexed,
and docketed with the most scrupulous care,
and his autographs are miracles of clearness
and musical calligraphy. His wife once said
to the present writer : " You may say what
you like about his music ; but if you don't
praise his handwriting he will be cross with
you." He dashes off his songs at great speed ;
often he has composed and written a whole
song during the intervals between the acts of
an opera he is conducting ; but he never works
at his larger works at odd moments. ' His usual
plan is to compose in the country in the
summer ; formerly it was at Marquardtstein,
now it is in his new house, which is still
more solitary, near Garmisch, so solitary, that
he whimsically said building operations were
interfered with by the chamois which came to
inspect the site. His method is to allow
himself a complete rest for a few weeks
and then to begin regular work. He retires
every day immediately after breakfast, which
is early, and the writing of necessary letters,

to a summer-house, where he remains undis-
turbed, even by telegrams or urgent messages,
till the midday meal, after which he reads or
walks for the rest of the day. Then, when he
returns to Berlin, he completes the scoring.
Every evening, when he is not conducting at
the Opera or elsewhere, he sits at his table
from about nine till one, never later ; and in
this way he gets through a vast amount of
work. The score of a Symphonic Poem used
to take him not more than three to four
months, and there is hardly an erasure or cor-
rection in it. The manuscript of his first childish
composition is as legible and as free from
alteration as those of his latest works.

Strauss is very sociable, but not in any sense
a society man. His favourite amusement is
skat, at which he is a great expert ; and he is
almost as proud of his reputation as one of the
best skat players in Germany as of his musical
fame. Being himself a man of very wide
culture, he loves the society of his intellectual
equals, and his house in Berlin is the resort of
all who are associated with the most advanced
movements in art. He is modern in all his
artistic tastes, as the pictures on his walls

testify. This love of all that is new and of this century is part and parcel of himself, and is not a mere accidental accretion, as some would have us believe. He is a convinced believer in the Übermensch, and respects all who, though they may be his opponents, display the qualities connoted by this word. Hence his admiration for the German Emperor, who is, intellectually and artistically, at the opposite pole, and though they can never agree on any musical topic. The relationship between the two is well characterized by an anecdote which may be given here for the sake of completeness, though it is very familiar. After a performance of an opera of Gluck the Emperor asked Strauss whether he did not think such music vastly superior to modern music-drama. When he said that he could hardly be expected to agree to such sentiments, the Emperor turned to the rest of the company and said : " See what a snake I have been warming in my bosom ! " After that Strauss was for some time known in Berlin as the " Hofbusenschlange " (i.e. Court Bosom Snake).

One trait in Strauss's character impresses itself on those who see him at close quarters on

important occasions, and that is his extraordinary power of keeping, or seeming to keep,
absolutely calm when everybody else is on
tenterhooks.ˆ Of course, it is only by dint of a
considerable effort of will that he manages it,
but it is none the less striking to see him in
the artists' room at a concert, when some
work of his has thrown a large audience into
a ferment of excitement, sitting down and
talking about things in general as if the whole
business had no further concern for him. On
these occasions he often finds an outlet for
his superfluous vitality by sitting down and
working steadily through the large pile of
autograph albums which generally await him.

There is no point at which he has been more
fiercely attacked than his relation to the
material rewards of his art. It is very difficult
to clear one's mind of cant on this matter, and
it is fatally easy to obtain unthinking applause
(from the very people who pride themselves
on the superiority of their intellect) by raising
this cry of "commercialism." Strauss is, at any
rate, quite frank, and without holding a brief
on one side or the other, one will do well to
consider his view of the question. He always

says that he is anxious, as quickly as the fates will allow, to acquire a capital which will enable him to live without holding any official post and devote himself to composition and literature. He does not say what the amount is to be, but presumably it is a fairly large one. It must be remembered that he was born with a wealthy grandfather, and has been used to comfortable — nay, luxurious — surroundings from his childhood. This is no more his fault than it is the fault of other composers that their grandfathers were poor or worthless. Besides, other musicians have had parents connected with business or finance, and have inherited business instincts. One would have more respect for the outcry against Strauss's monetary successes if one had any sort of confidence that those who protest most vehemently would ever refuse a good fee if they had the chance. Not that they are to blame ; for it is difficult to see why musicians, of all people, should be expected to do everything for the love of Art or the good of mankind. It is all very well, too, to hold up one's hands in horror because Strauss was paid £1750 for the *Domestic Symphony* and say that Beethoven got a paltry twenty pounds for a great symphony, or to simulate noble indignation because *Salome* brings in so many hundreds a year. Those who pay him have not been the losers, at any rate, and do not complain.· On the other hand, he sold *Traum durch die Dämmerung* for thirty shillings, and the publisher is said to have made £400 out of it in the first two years. Besides, after all, the unholy profits of the *Domestic Symphony* and *Salome* combined will probably never amount to a tenth part of those won by *Soldiers in the Park* or *The Merry Widow Waltz*. One of the favourite weapons used against him has been that he once in America conducted a concert in a room above a large store in the afternoon while the ordinary business of the establishment was going on downstairs. "Prostitution of Art" was the politest thing said about it. The attack has been renewed within the last few weeks, and he was induced to reply, and what he said is instructive. He said that, as a matter of fact, the room was, or was turned into, an excellent concert room with very good acoustic properties, and that it was stipulated beforehand that all traces of business should be removed. Further, he had one of the best orchestras in the States at his disposal, and better opportunities for rehearsal than were granted by some of the most prominent artistic institutions. Even if this had not been so, he continues, he might well say, as was said by an eminent actress who was taken to task for appearing in a hippodrome : " Where I appear, there it is a first-class theatre."

Every composer of any importance is accused of not doing enough to help his less prosperous colleagues, and of jealousy of those equally successful. Strauss has not escaped, and the charge is as true, or untrue, in his case as in most others. But all English people should remember with gratitude his almost impassioned advocacy of Elgar in the days when England had not yet learned to admire the *Dream of Gerontius*. His remarks in his speech at the banquet after the Lower Rhenish Festival at Düsseldorf in 1902 were no mere idle after-dinner talk. He spoke them knowing full well that they were, in a sense, spoken *ex cathedrâ*, and that they would be severely criticized by his German colleagues as unpatriotic. At that time hardly any English authority had dared to speak so enthusiastically of Elgar and his work.

In appearance Strauss is scrupulously neat always—not in the least like the traditional musician—without being in any sense fashionable, and his face is quite unlike that of any other great composer. Indeed, some of his critics have been heard to say that there could be no real music behind a forehead so round and prominent. In his speech he clings tenaciously to the broad Doric of his native Munich ; and though (in *Feuersnot*) he has been the partner in a violent satire on his fellow-townsmen, he resents attacks on them from other quarters, especially from North Germans. The typical Bavarian naturally looks on the average Prussian much as a Home Rule M.P. looks on the " garrison " of Dublin Castle ; and though Strauss is too diplomatic to say much, his friends would not be surprised to hear that he agreed with his legendary fellow-countryman who said that Berlin would be beautiful if there were not so many Prussians in it.

ALFRED KALISCH

CONTENTS

ILLUSTRATIONS

RICHARD STRAUSS

CHAPTER I

LIFE

RICHARD STRAUSS has for so long been the subject of heated discussion in the musical circles of two continents that it is hard to realize that he has not yet attained his forty-fourth year. Thirteen years ago, at an age when Beethoven had got only as far as his unadventurous first symphony, and Wagner was merely laying the foundations of his style in " Rienzi " and " The Flying Dutchman," Strauss's *Till Eulenspiegel* and *Also sprach Zarathustra* had already marked him out as a revolutionary of the most daring type ; and one needs only to recall the titles of some of his later works—*Don Quixote, Ein Heldenleben,* the *Symphonia Domestica,* and *Salome*—to be

B

reminded that around each of them has raged
a critical battle as furious as any that was
fought about the maturer works of Wagner.
He has often been as unfortunate in his friends
as he has been fortunate in his enemies ; he
has been foolishly abused by critics of the
type of the late Eduard Hanslick, whose con-
demnation of any piece of modern music could
almost be taken as a certificate of its excel-
lence ; and he has been admired with equal
foolishness by others, who were wilfully blind
to some of the serious defects of his work, but
who used him as a stick with which to beat
a contrasted form of art which they disliked.
All this commotion at least testifies to Strauss's
significance in the history of music, for the
whole musical world does not form itself into
two armed camps, breathing fire and slaughter
at each other, over any man of less than first-
rate importance.   And a rough measure of
the effect he makes even on those who dislike
him most may be had in the violence of the
epithets they hurl at his head, some of which
take us back to the good old days when the
" Meistersinger " overture was called " an ugly
riot of dissonance," and the opera itself " a

RICHARD STRAUSS AND HIS MOTHER

boneless tone mollusc," and when " Parsifal "
reminded delicate-souled German critics of
" the howls of a dog undergoing vivisection."
To the expert in the history of journalistic
objurgation, epithets of this kind tell their own
tale ; if a bundle of them, relating to some
one of whom he otherwise knew nothing, were
brought to him, he could almost reconstruct
the artist from them as a scientist can reconstruct the form of an animal from the evidence
of a few scattered bones. When a certain
dramatic critic, for example, called Ibsen
" a muck-ferreting dog," the skilled in these
matters, hearing the phrase and knowing the
critical record of the author of it, could at
once understand the ideals of Ibsen without
the necessity of reading a line of him. And
when we find Strauss being thrown into the
same plague-pit with Ibsen and other moderns,
and the same kind of burial service being
imprecated over him, that in itself is enough
to prove his main offence to be that he is a
progressive, and so to arouse the sympathy of
many people for him. No one has yet compiled a Straussean *Schimpflexikon* on the lines
of the one that was compiled about Wagner,

—an entertaining collection of all the terms of abuse that have been showered upon him ; but when it is compiled it will make agreeable reading for posterity. Already we can smile at some of the earlier judgments upon Strauss. From a book published by a well-known American critic only four years ago I cull the following choice cauliflowers of rhetoric, all prompted, be it observed, by three of Strauss's early works that are now accepted in every concert room as blandly as the " Tannhäuser " overture, *Tod und Verklärung, Don Juan,* and *Till Eulenspiegel.* The last-named, according to our critic, is " a study in musical depiction of wandering vulgarity, of jocular obscenity, a vast and coruscating jumble of instrumental cackles about things unfit to be mentioned . . . With Ibsens, Maeterlincks, and Strausses," the indignant prophet goes on, writing with his foot on the loud pedal all the time, " plucking like soulless ghouls upon the snapping heartstrings of humanity, treating the heart as a monochord for the scientific measurement of intervals of pain, and finally poking with their skeleton fingers in the ashes of the tomb to see if they could not find a single smouldering ember of human agony, we had attained a rare state of morbidity in art. We felt that when art had turned for her inspiration to the asylum, the brothel, and the pest-house, it was time for a new renaissance." It is hinted that some of the material of *Don Juan* and *Till Eulenspiegel* is " unfit for publication." Still beating the big drum in the interests of musical sanitation, much as the priests in the Middle Ages used to scare away evil spirits by ringing the church bells noisily, our author goes on to say that with Strauss " the orchestra is transformed into a psychoscope, and the symphony is become a treatise on mental diseases and methods of conversing with the dead." " The modern ear," in fact, " is suffering from acute myringomycrosis, a cheerful affliction caused by the growth of fungi on the ear drum." We read of " the chortling barbarians of the Strauss phantasy," who are separated from other and more civilized beings by a " vast and impassable gulf of fetid inspiration." Strauss is leading music along a path that can only finish " in the corruption and rank odour of the morgue." And becoming a little incoherent, as prophets

are apt to do when their rhetoric gets into
their head, our author has a final fling at
" *Till Eulenspiegel*, Gargantua of Germany,
noisome, nasty, rollicking *Till*, with the
whirligig scale of a yellow clarinet in his
brain and the beer-house rhythm of a pint pot
in his heart." And yet schoolgirls listen with
enjoyment to these foul and pestilential works,
and, what is worse, take their mothers to hear
them !

This wild and malodorous language, taken
from an essay by a critic who can write sen-
sibly enough on other topics, is quoted here
not so much for its own sake as to give the
reader an idea of the frenzy of opposition
that Strauss raises in some worthy minds.
As I have said, the very violence of the language is in itself an evidence of the disturbing
effect he has had upon modern music and
musicians ; the pole must have gone very
deep into the stagnant pond to bring so much
mud as this to the surface. And the peculiar
wording of the charges against Strauss indi-
cates the new impulses he has brought into
music. When dramatic critics of a certain
type accuse a new author of immorality we

may be sure that all he has really done is to be deeply moved by certain sad aspects of human nature and human life, and to try to communicate to his fellow-men his own sense of the pity that such evil should be. And when composers like Wagner and Strauss are accused of outraging humanity in their music, we may be sure that it is only because they have felt more of the sting or the sweetness or the humour of life than their forerunners did, and have tried to express it all in their music. We are not at present, be it noted, passing any judgment, favourable or unfavourable, upon the actual work of Strauss. That work must finally stand or fall in virtue of what it does, not in virtue of what it aims at doing ; that is to say, if the expression itself is false or the architecture bad, the composer cannot fall back upon a plea of good intentions. It may be a desirable thing to bring music into closer touch with actual life than the great classical masters have done—that line of development, indeed, was one that music was bound to follow in our own day ; but if the work is not beautifully conceived and strongly wrought it will

not endure. The men who lead the multitude
to a new Pisgah do not always enter the pro-
mised land themselves. They may live in
history, as Liszt, for example, does, less for
what they have achieved than for what they
have made it possible, by flinging open the
gates, for other people to achieve. The
opinion of those who regard Strauss as merely
a charlatan and a poseur, a self-conscious
manufacturer of ugliness and eccentricity,
may be put aside as not worth consideration.
But those who are sympathetically interested
in his work and in the musical development
for which it stands may reasonably ask
whether he is one of the great creators or only
one of the great emancipators ; whether his
music will keep its interest for the ear and
the soul of future generations, or will simply,
like that of Monteverde or that of Philipp
Emanuel Bach, be a historical link between
two greater phases of musical thought. This
question has, in fact, been asked by many
thoughtful observers. In the following pages
we shall try to see which way the evidence
points.

Strauss's father, Franz Strauss (born 26 February, 1822), was the first horn player in the Munich Court Orchestra, and the author of several studies for the instrument. He was an artist of exceptional ability, and specially famous for the beauty of his phrasing. " My father," Richard Strauss once said, " was, as regards beauty and volume of tone, perfection of phrasing, and technique, one of the most notable of horn players." In the light of the revolutionary tendencies exhibited by his son, it is interesting to learn that Franz Strauss was an orthodox conservative musician, who never got over his early anti-Wagnerian bias. Wagner himself was well aware of this bias, and once, it is said, after a performance of one of his operas, in which the hornist had played even more exquisitely than usual, remarked banteringly that Strauss could not have played the music so beautifully had he been a real anti-Wagnerian ; to which Strauss merely replied doggedly that " that had nothing to do with it." He married Josephine, the daughter of Georg Pschorr, the well-known brewer of Munich beer. Their son Richard was born 11 June, 1864 ; a younger sister, Johanna, to whom some of the composer's works are dedicated, came into the world 9 June, 1867.

Richard's musical ability showed itself at a very early age. He had already begun to play the piano at four, his mother being his first tutor ; at six he composed a " Schneider-polka " in the accommodating key of C major, —his tiny brain probably being unequal at the time to the strain of flats and sharps,—and a Christmas song. From 1870–1874 he attended an elementary school at Munich ; here he worked hard at the technique of the piano and at that of the violin. In 1874 he entered at the Gymnasium, where he remained until 1882. From there he proceeded to the University of Munich, leaving this, however, in the following year. In the midst of his other studies he was receiving a careful musical education. From 1875 to 1880 he had a thorough grounding in harmony, counterpoint, and instrumentation from Hofkapell-meister F. W. Meyer, to whom later on he dedicated the Serenade for wind instruments that was published as opus 7. In the next compositions of his of which we hear, the pale

domestic glories of the " Schneiderpolka " and
the Christmas song are left far behind; we
read of a chorus from the " Electra " of Sopho-
cles and a " Festival Chorus " being performed
at a " Prüfungs-Konzert " at the Gymnasium.
By the time he had reached his sixteenth year
he had become something of a public character.
In 1880 a singer at the Munich opera, Frau
Meysenheim, sang three of his songs in public.
On 16 March, 1881, the Benno Walter Quartet,
at one of their concerts, played his String
Quartet in A major (op. 2) ; while on the
30th of the same month Hermann Levi gave
a performance of his Symphony in D minor,
a work in four movements, that has hitherto
remained unpublished. All this while his
training, as any one, indeed, can see from his
early compositions, had been on severely
orthodox lines. Strauss himself has told us
that until 1885, when he made the acquaintance of Alexander Ritter, he had been "brought
up in a strictly classical way," on nothing but
Haydn, Mozart, and Beethoven, and that only
after 1885 did he attain, viâ Mendelssohn, to
Chopin and Schumann, and then to Brahms.
The evidence of this is writ large on all his

earlier works : the *Fünf Clavierstücke*, op. 3
(1881) ; the Pianoforte Sonata, op. 5 (1881) ;
the Sonata for Violoncello and Piano, op. 6
(1882–3) ; the Serenade for wind instruments,
op. 7 (1882–3) ; the Violin Concerto, op. 8
(1882–3) ; the "Stimmungsbilder" for piano,
op. 9 (1882–3) ; and the Concerto for French
horn, op. 11 (1883–4).

After leaving the University Strauss spent
the winter of 1883–4 in Berlin, where, as at
Munich, he was unusually fortunate in getting
his youthful works performed. A Concert
Overture in C minor (still unpublished) was
played by the Court Orchestra under Radecke.
In Berlin he attracted the attention of Hans
von Bülow, who conceived for the young man
one of those sudden enthusiasms in which the
career of Bülow was so prolific. He placed
Strauss's Serenade on the programmes of his
tour with the Meiningen Orchestra. Besides
encouraging Strauss as a composer, he seems
to have realized that he had a gift for conducting. In the spring of 1885, at Bülow's invita-
tion, Strauss conducted, at a concert of the
Meiningen Orchestra in Munich, a four-move-
ment Suite of his own for wind instruments,

that has not yet been published.* He gave it without any rehearsal, a fact which points to unusual confidence on Bülow's part, either in Strauss or, which is more probable, in the wind players of his orchestra. Bülow, however, had evidently a high opinion of the young man, for on 1 October of the same year he engaged him as assistant " Musikdirektor " under himself at Meiningen. Here Strauss played, under the conductorship of Bülow, the C minor Pianoforte Concerto of Mozart, and conducted his own Symphony in F minor (op. 12), which had been written in 1883–4, and of which the first performance had been given in New York on 13 December, 1884, by Theodore Thomas. His other compositions of this period include the Piano Quartet (op. 13), written in 1883–4—with which he won the prize offered by the Berlin Tonkünstler-Verein—and the *Wandrers Sturmlied* (1884–5). Although what we now regard as the real

* "This," says Mr. James Huneker in his article on Strauss in "Overtones," "must be the grand Suite in B flat, misleadingly numbered opus 14, the same opus number as the *Sturmlied*. It is scored for thirteen wind instruments, and has been heard in London. The introduction and entire fourth movement are said to be the best. It is early Strauss."

Strauss had not yet appeared in his music, the style of the young man of twenty, as shown in the Symphony in F minor, the Piano Quartet, and the *Wandrers Sturmlied*, had changed considerably from that of the composer of the still earlier works. In these three works, and more especially in the *Wandrers Sturmlied*, most people see the influence of Brahms, in whom Bülow had probably interested him. A still stronger influence was now to come into his life. According to Strauss himself the turning-point of his career was his friendship with Alexander Ritter (1833–96), a man of many parts—violinist, composer, *littérateur*, and music-seller. One of Strauss's German biographers, Dr. Erich Urban, thinks that the part played by Ritter in the development of the composer has been exaggerated ; at most, he thinks, Ritter could only have given the final impulse to tendencies that had long been slumbering in Strauss. Ritter, he says, was " ein verworrener Denker, ein unklarer Kopf " (" a confused thinker, an unclear intelligence "). He holds that it was more probably Bülow who applied the torch of modernity to Strauss's

smouldering faculties ; and he quotes a remark of the composer to the effect that in
October, 1885, he attended daily the rehearsals
of the Meiningen Orchestra, at which he was
initiated by Bülow into the art of conducting
" in his [Bülow's] sense and in that of Wagner." We may take it for granted that
Bülow brought the young composer into closer
touch with many of the main currents of
modern music. At the same time we are
bound to accept Strauss's own declaration
of how much he owed to Ritter. He was,
according to Strauss, a well-read man, par-
ticularly in philosophy. He had married a
niece of Wagner, and was an ardent apostle
of the ideas of Wagner and Liszt and the so-
called " New German " school, with its ideal
of " Musik als Ausdruck." " His influence,"
says Strauss, " was in the nature of the storm-
wind. He urged me on to the development
of the poetic, the expressive in music, as
exemplified in the works of Liszt, Wagner,
and Berlioz. My symphonic fantasia, *Aus
Italien*, is the connecting link between the
old and the new methods." Erich Urban,
however, doggedly declines to see any in-

fluence of Ritter in *Aus Italien*, the *Burleske*, the Violin Sonata (op. 18), or the six songs that form op. 19.

When Bülow left Meiningen, in November, 1885, Strauss became his successor. He occupied this post until 1 April, 1886. The April and May of that year he spent mostly in Rome and Naples ; it was from this Italian journey that *Aus Italien* (op. 16) sprang. The work was first performed at Munich, in the spring of 1887, under Strauss himself. On 1 August, 1886, he was appointed third Kapellmeister at the Munich Opera, under Levi and Fischer, a position he gave up on 31 July, 1889. On 1 October, 1889, he became assistant Kapellmeister at Weimar, under Lassen. By this time he had " found himself " as a composer, as the bare enumeration of the works written between 1885 and 1889 will show. *Aus Italien* was followed in 1886 by the six songs published as op. 17, the first of which— " Seitdem dein Aug' in meines schaute," with its more refined passion and its greater freedom of handling—has only to be compared with one of the earlier songs, such as the popular " Zueignung " of op. 10, for the

RICHARD STRAUSS AS A CHILD

difference between the Strauss of eighteen
and the Strauss of twenty-two—the pre-
Ritter and the post-Ritter Strauss—to be at
once apparent. In 1887 came the vigorous
Violin Sonata (op. 18), which, youthful as it
still is in comparison with Strauss's later work,
inhabits a different world from the Violin
Concerto of 1882–3 (op. 8). Passing over the
songs of op. 19 (1887), op. 21 (1888), and op.
22 (1886–7), it need only be mentioned that
op. 20 was the tone-poem *Don Juan* (1888,
first performance in Berlin under Bülow),
op. 23, *Macbeth*,* and op. 24, *Tod und Verklärung* (1889, first performance Eisenach,
1890), for it to be quite evident that in the
two or three years immediately succeeding
1885 Strauss had left far behind him the sober
classical ideals of his boyhood, and was well
on the way to becoming the audacious revolutionary who so startled the musical world
between 1895—the year of *Till Eulenspiegel*—
and 1898—the year of *Ein Heldenleben*.

* *Macbeth*, though it bears a later opus number than
Don Juan, is in reality Strauss's first tone-poem. It was
written in the summer of 1887, and given under Bülow
in Berlin, then revised, and published after *Don Juan*. It
was first performed in Weimar in 1890 in its revised form.

C

On leaving Munich, in October, 1889, as
we have seen, Strauss went to Weimar, where
he remained as conductor until the beginning
of June, 1894. Among the operas he produced there were two short works of his
mentor, Alexander Ritter—" Der faule Hans "
and " Wem die Krone ? "—while as conductor
of the Liszt Society at Leipzig he did a good
deal for modern music. Meanwhile he had
made his first experiment in opera. An in-
flammation of the lungs and a general break-
down through overwork had sent him, in the
spring of 1892, on a year's tour to Greece,
Egypt, and Sicily in search of health. At
Cairo, on 29 December, 1892, he began the
first act of *Guntram*, finishing it at Luxor on
27 February of the following year. The
second act was completed at Villa Blandini,
Ramacca, Sicily, on 4 June, 1893 ; and the
third at Marquartstein, Upper Bavaria, on
5 September, 1893. Strauss himself conducted
the first performance at Weimar, on 12 May,
1894. Heinrich Zeller was the Guntram, and
Pauline de Ahna—the daughter of the Bavarian
general Adolf de Ahna,—who later on became
the wife of the composer, was the Freihild. The

work had no great success with the public,
partly, no doubt, because of the palpable
traces of Wagner in both the music and the
libretto, which latter, by the way, is Strauss's
own.

From Weimar he returned in October, 1894,
to Munich, this time as first Kapellmeister.
During the winter of 1894–5 he also conducted
the Berlin Philharmonic concerts in succession
to Bülow, while in the summer of 1894 he had
conducted the first performance of *Tannhäuser*
that had ever been given at Bayreuth. Pauline
de Ahna, whom he married shortly afterwards,
was the Elisabeth. The years that followed
were busy ones for Strauss. In 1895 he conducted concerts in Budapest, Leipzig, and
other towns ; in 1896 and 1897 he conducted
at Brussels, Moscow, etc., and at the Düsseldorf Festival ; in 1897 he visited Amsterdam,
London, Barcelona, Brussels, Hamburg, and
Paris ; and in 1898 Zurich and Madrid. In
October, 1898, he left Munich to take up the
post, which he yet holds, of conductor at the
Berlin Royal Opera. His duties at Weimar,
Munich, and Berlin necessarily brought him
into contact with music of all schools, and it

is satisfactory to note that he can conduct
a trifle like the " Fledermaus " of the younger
Johann Strauss with the same gusto as " Tristan " or " Die Meistersinger " or " The Barber
of Baghdad." The catholicity of his taste is
further shown by the fact that he was one of
the first to see the beauty of Humperdinck's
" Hänsel und Gretel," and the first to give that
delightful work to the world, in December, 1893,
during his Kapellmeistership at Weimar. As
he was at that time thinking out his *Also sprach
Zarathustra*, which, all things considered, is
the most revolutionary work of our generation,
it is evident that the most intense absorption
in his own intellectual world is not incompatible
with the warmest sympathy with musicians
of radically different outlooks.

In the midst of all the heavy work entailed
by this conducting and travelling he found
time to write that series of orchestral works
which defined once for all his position in the
history of the music of the nineteenth century.
Till Eulenspiegel (op. 28) followed close upon
the heels of *Guntram ;* it was written in 1894,
and received its first performance at Cologne,
under Wüllner, in 1895. From there it

quickly made its way to almost every musical city in Germany—except his birthplace, Munich. Only two songs separate *Till Eulenspiegel* from *Also sprach Zarathustra* (op. 30), which was first performed under Strauss himself at Frankfort, on 27 November, 1895. *Don Quixote* (op. 35) followed in 1897, and *Ein Heldenleben* (op. 40) in 1898 ; and at the age of thirty-four Strauss was the most talked-of musician in the world. He had already carried the typical modern art-form, the symphonic poem, as far beyond anything of the kind that his predecessors had written, as Wagner in *Tristan* had swung himself beyond the ken of all earlier or contemporary composers of opera. His nine following opus numbers comprise nothing but songs and a few male-voice choruses. His next large work was the opera *Feuersnoth* (op. 50), produced at Dresden on 21 November, 1901. This was succeeded by " Das Tal " (op. 51), a song for bass voice and orchestra, and a choral work, *Taillefer* (op. 52) ; then, in 1904, came the much-discussed *Symphonia Domestica* (op. 53, first performance in New York, 21 March, 1904, under Strauss). One would have thought

that the climax of excitement about him had
been reached long ago, but the production of
his third opera, *Salome* (op. 54), in Dresden,
on 9 December, 1905, roused a fiercer storm
of controversy than ever. Since *Salome* he
has produced nothing on a large scale. Opus 55
is a *Bardengesang* (1906) for male-voice chorus
and orchestra ; op. 56 a set of six songs ;
and op. 57 two marches. A fourth opera,
Electra, has not yet seen the light.

Strauss's personal acquaintance with England dates from 1897. August Manns had
already given his *Till Eulenspiegel* at the
Crystal Palace on 21 March, 1896, and *Also
sprach Zarathustra* on 6 March, 1897. On
7 December, 1897, at a Wagner concert given
by Mr. Schulz-Curtius in the Queen's Hall,
London, Strauss conducted his own *Till
Eulenspiegel* and *Tod und Verklärung*, this
being the first English performance of the
latter work. His music, however, spread
slowly here ; even in November, 1902, the
" Musical Times " could say, with unconscious
irony, that " the name of Richard Strauss is
gradually becoming known in England." On
1 February, 1902, the love-scene from *Feuers-*

noth was given by Mr. Wood at Queen's Hall.

Some months later, at the Lower Rhenish Festival, held at Düsseldorf in May, Strauss had made a remark that had unexpectedly wide-reaching consequences. Elgar's *Gerontius* had just received, under the baton of Julius Buths, a performance that made amends for the inadequate rendering it had had at the Birmingham Festival of 1900. After the official toasts had all been proposed Strauss surprised every one by spontaneously proposing another; " I raise my glass," he said, " to the welfare and success of the first English Progressivist, Meister Edward Elgar, and of the young progressive school of English composers." The remark gave great offence in some quarters in England, where several estimable composers, who were, however, neither progressive nor Meisters, felt that the compliment to Elgar was a backhander to themselves. But Strauss's generous words undoubtedly had much to do with the revival of Elgar's great work in this country. At the end of the same month and the beginning of June, Strauss gave some concerts in London in conjunction with Herr von Possart, who recited Tennyson's " Enoch Arden," the composer at the piano accompanying with his own music (op. 38). Performances were also given, under Strauss, of *Tod und Verklärung, Don Juan, Till Eulenspiegel,* and the Violin Sonata. On 12 December, 1902, Mr. Wood gave the first English performance of *Ein Heldenleben.* The critics, where they were not dubious as to the value of the new work, were mostly rather hostile ; but the public took to it, and Mr. Wood repeated it on 1 January and 28 March, 1903.

In September, 1902, *Tod und Verklärung* was given at the Worcester Festival, this being the first performance of any work of his at an English festival. The *Sturmlied* was given at the Sheffield Festival in October of the same year.

In June, 1903, an elaborate Strauss festival, lasting three days, was held in London. The fine Amsterdam Orchestra had been engaged ; it had the reputation of playing Strauss's works with especial brilliancy, and *Ein Heldenleben* had been dedicated to its conductor, Wilhelm Mengelberg. Two performances were

RICHARD STRAUSS AS A BOY

given of *Also sprach Zarathustra,* two of *Till Eulenspiegel,* two of *Ein Heldenleben,* one of *Tod und Verklärung,* one of *Don Juan,* one of *Macbeth,* and one of *Don Quixote,* Strauss and Mengelberg sharing the work of conducting. Two movements from *Aus Italien* were also given. Mr. Wilhelm Backhaus played the solo part in the *Burleske,* Mr. John Harrison sang excerpts from *Guntram,* and the composer's wife and Mr. Ffrangcon Davies sang a number of his songs. The Festival was not a financial success, but it was widely discussed, and did much to establish Strauss firmly in the English concert room. Since then his orchestral compositions have figured regularly on both London and provincial programmes, and his larger new works, with the exception, of course, of the operas, have been heard here fairly promptly. *Taillefer* was given at the Bristol Festival of October, 1905, and the *Symphonia Domestica* received its first English performance under Mr. Wood, on 25 February, 1905. *Don Quixote,* too, has been repeated in London, though not in the provinces ; and Strauss himself has paid this country more than one visit since 1903. *Salome,* presum-

ably, we shall never hear on the stage in
England ; but the dance from it was played
by the New Symphony Orchestra, under
Mr. Fritz Cassirer, at Queen's Hall on 22
November, 1907. At a concert to be given at
Queen's Hall on 19 March of the present year
it was intended that Strauss should conduct
the dance and two long vocal excerpts from
Salome,—the great scene between Salome and
Jochanaan, and the final scene of the opera ;
but the concert fell through owing to a dis-
agreement between the Queen's Hall authori-
ties and the German " Genossenschaft " that
manages the financial affairs of the composers
belonging to it.

It will be seen that Strauss's life, so far as
external events are concerned, has been
comparatively uneventful ; it is mainly a
record of strenuous labour as composer and
conductor. When we survey the already
enormous mass of his music we feel that this
alone is enough work for one man to have
done ; and when we think of the further
great strain upon his time and his strength
involved in his constant conducting and his
travelling—for he has toured the world from

New York to Moscow—we wonder that he
has not broken down long ago. Fortunately
for him he keeps clear, for the most part, of
the literary side of music. He has edited
a German edition of Berlioz's " Treatise on
Instrumentation," has written a magazine
article or two, and is the editor of a little
series of books—" Die Musik " is the general
title of the series—most of which would be
highly interesting if only the atrocious German
typography of them permitted any one who
respects his eyesight to read them. The
latest volume of the series is upon Strauss's
old friend, Alexander Ritter ; the author is
Siegmund von Hausegger.

Of Strauss as a conductor only those who
have heard him frequently, and in all kinds of
music, have a right to speak. The readings
he has given of his own works in England
have been highly personal ; in *Also sprach
Zarathustra* and *Ein Heldenleben*, for example,
he stresses the occasional freakishnesses of the
music more than the majority of other con-
ductors do. In his operatic conducting, however, he is said to pay less attention to detail
and more to breadth of general effect ; and it

is claimed for him that he is both broad in his sympathies and conscientious in the discharge of his duties, giving the same care, for example, to an opera by Lortzing as he does to one by Wagner.

CHAPTER II

IT is generally agreed that the Strauss we know to-day dates from *Aus Italien* (op. 16) ; and though all divisions of this kind are necessarily somewhat arbitrary, it will be found convenient for purposes of criticism to draw a line of demarcation there. The year of composition of his first opus, the *Festmarsch*, is apparently not definitely known, but assuming it to be about 1880, the works to be considered in this chapter cover a period of about five years, from 1880 to 1885, in which latter year Strauss would still be only twenty-one. They include thirteen songs—the consideration of which we may reserve for the chapter on his songs as a whole—two Quartets, ten small pieces for pianoforte, a Pianoforte Sonata, a Sonata for Violoncello and Piano, a Concerto for Violin and Orchestra, a Concerto

for the French Horn, a large choral and orchestral work, a Serenade for wind instruments, a March for Orchestra, and a Symphony.
The general impression one gets from all these
works is that of a head full to overflowing with
music, a temperament that is energetic and
forthright rather than warm, a faculty—unusual in so young a composer—of keeping the
hearer's attention almost always engaged, and
a general lack not only of young-mannish
sentimentality, but of sentiment. There is
often a good deal of ardour in the writing,
but it is the ardour of the intellect rather than
of the emotions. Though he is sometimes
dry, he is scarcely ever dull ; the dryness is
a personal tang ; it suggests a sinewy young
athlete's joy in his own energizing and in his
freedom from anything like excess of feeling.
The work is the outcome of a definite personality, not the mere music-making of a man who
has nothing of his own to say. It is this youthful strength that makes the best of the earlier
works still interesting and enjoyable. Even
in the boyish *Festmarsch* (op. 1) there is a
quite amazing vigour of the bantam kind ;
and even in the Trio, with its amusingly self-

confident little melody, that reminds one of
the " cheekiness " of some healthy and irre-
pressible urchin, there is unexpected energy.
The first, second, and fourth movements of
the String Quartet (op. 2) have the same breezy,
healthy quality. We see it again in Nos. 2,
4, and 5 of the *Fünf Klavierstücke* (op. 3), and
in all the fast movements of the Piano Quartet
(op. 13), the Violin Concerto (op. 8), the
Violoncello Sonata (op. 6), the Piano Sonata
(op. 5), and the Symphony (op. 12). The
music here is generally, in spite of its untiring
energy of movement, a little hard and metallic ;
it reminds us of arabesques traced on steel.
On the other hand, wherever the youthful
Strauss has to sing rather than declaim, when
he has to be emotional rather than intellectual,
as in his slow movements, he almost invariably
fails. At best, as in Nos. 1 and 3 of the *Fünf
Klavierstücke,* he manages to echo the sentiment of some previous composer—Schumann
in the first case, Beethoven in the second.
Schumann's romanticism is written all over
No. 1, and the middle section in particular has
come straight from the G minor section of the
" Humoreske " ; while in No. 3 there is a

rather conscious imitation of the Beethoven
funeral march manner. There is Schumann
again in the andantino " Träumerei " of the
Stimmungsbilder for pianoforte, as, indeed,
there is almost throughout the series, though
it must be said that the music is not weakly
imitative. It still has the peculiar firmness
and confidence of style that was so characteristic of Strauss from the outset ; he was never
in the least danger of becoming one of the
ordinary sentimental Schumannikins. In the
slow movements of the String Quartet, the
Piano Sonata, the Violoncello Sonata, the
Violin Concerto, and the Symphony he is
obviously ill at ease. He feels it hard to
squeeze a tear out of his unclouded young eyes,
to make those taut, whip-cord young nerves
of his quiver with emotion. Sometimes he
comes near the commonplace, which is a rare
thing for him ; for however one may dislike
this or that phrase of Strauss one can rarely
despise it. In the Violin Concerto and the
Violoncello Sonata he wisely cuts the slow
movement as short as possible, and gets on to
his finale or his rondo with an evident sigh
of relief ; in the Piano Sonata he dovetails

into the centre of the slow movement a playful
scherzo-like section. In his rapid movements
the rhythmic interest is always well main-
tained, and the curve of the phrase, if not
sensuously beautiful or captivating, is at any
rate lithe and muscular ; but in his andantes
he usually falls into a rather obvious rhythmic
swing, and he shows more immaturity and
less resource in his accompaniments here than
elsewhere, one noticeable mannerism being the
syncopations that often underlie the theme.

It is hard to say what would have become
of Strauss had he chosen to continue working
in the abstract classical forms instead of the
modern poetic forms which he adopted after
Aus Italien. Sometimes, in the very early
works, he rather loses himself in the development portions, which of course are the test
of a composer's power of continuous and logical
thinking ; he is inclined to swagger his way
through a difficulty rather than to solve it.
At other times he shows a faculty for compact
weaving that makes us think that had he
cultivated the traditional symphonic form a
few years longer he might have achieved something notable in it. Even in the first move-

D

ment of the Piano Sonata, written when he was only sixteen or seventeen, there is, in spite of an obvious discontinuity of idea now and then, at times a quite surprising strength and consistency of tissue.* Perhaps the extraordinary nervous force of Strauss's later compositions and the audacity of their form make us too prone to underestimate the value of his earliest works. When we try to look impartially at things like the Symphony, the Piano Quartet, and the *Burleske*, we recognize in them the possibility of a first-rate symphonist. Nothing can be further from the truth than the idea of Strauss—current in some quarters—as a harum-scarum young man whose fancy runs away with him for want of sufficient education in the principles of form to hold it in check. As a matter of fact, probably no young musician has ever had a more solid grounding in the accepted musical forms, or has practised them more easily. When he left the Munich Gymnasium

---

* The little hammering figure of four notes that runs through the greater part of the movement is obviously an echo of the "Fate" theme in Beethoven's fifth symphony. The vitality and freshness of Strauss's treatment of it are really astonishing.

in 1882, at the age of eighteen, according to Professor Giehrl every musician who knew him was " staggered " (" es sei für alle Musiker etwas geradezu Verblüffendes ") at the ease and completeness of his mastery of all the forms. It is not lack of command of the classical manner that has kept Strauss from working contentedly, like Brahms, within the frame of the Beethoven symphony, but the recognition that for ideas like his the classical manner is inappropriate. And in the works of his early manhood, written about 1884 and 1885, we can plainly see a contest going on within him between the dutiful youth who believes what his masters had told him, and the adventurous young man who is beginning to think for himself. The *Burleske* is an interesting example of this struggle. A good deal of it is undeniably Brahmsian in spirit, the beginning of the first theme for the piano being a reminiscence indeed, of the theme of Brahms's D minor Ballade; and the frequent cross-rhythms in the work have been openly bought at the Brahms counter. And yet the face of the Strauss we all know keeps peeping out of the

heavy Brahmsian hood like the face of Till
Eulenspiegel from under the hood of the
monk. Already we see he has the notion—
which later on he will often carry to an extreme
—that music can be made almost as definite
as words or pictures. He tells the pianist,
for example, to play a certain phrase in the
Burleske " con umore," without at the same
time telling him how to do it. The " humour "
obviously exists only in the mind of the composer, and in that of the pianist if he can
persuade himself that he sees it. The phrase
in itself is just mildly graceful, and it is safe
to say that not a single person who has heard
the *Burleske* has ever dreamt that it was
meant to be humorous. It is evident that if
Strauss was bent on trying to suggest things
of this kind in instrumental music, the classical
and abstract forms were not the place for
him ; the sooner he jumped the wall and got
into the field of programme music the better
for him and for us. There were other signs
that he was beginning to strain at the classical
leash. Perhaps, indeed, some of the earliest
works are not so innocently abstract as we
imagine. Even in the Violin Concerto (1882-3)

RICHARD STRAUSS AS A BOY

he interpolates the second subject of the first movement in the finale, thirty bars or so before the end, and marks it "molto con espressione," as if it had some poetic significance in his mind. In the Symphony (1883–4) both the third and fourth movements contain frequent reminiscences of the first, and one cannot doubt that the reappearances of the earlier themes are in obedience to some poetic scheme. It is thus probable that even the good boy whom Meyer and Giehrl were patting on the back for his touching filial devotion to the classical form was already hatching sinister plans for turning the old lady out of doors. Perhaps all that was needed to divert Strauss into the new path at this time was some over-mastering emotion which he would feel to be inexpressible in the older manner ; and of the coming of this there are signs in the works of the end of his first period. In the first and third movements of the Piano Quartet, in particular, there is a quite new note. There is all the old energy, but it is now touched and quickened by an unaccustomed emotion. The andante is the first slow movement of Strauss of which the fount and origin is pure spontaneous feeling—not the mask of feeling put on at the bidding of the intellect. Not only does the mood of this Piano Quartet often forecast that of *Aus Italien*, but the thematic phrases begin to show one marked characteristic of the style of the later Strauss—a superabundant energy that sends the melodies sweeping far up and down the scale, and a length of breath that enables them to run an exceptionally long course. Everything is ready for the re-birth of the real Strauss. He is an accomplished technician, he has complete mastery of his ideas, he is acquiring fresh emotional energy without losing any of his old intellectual energy; all that is needed now is to find some form that will give the freest play to the best that is in him. This form he ultimately found in programme music.

CHAPTER III

LATER INSTRUMENTAL WORKS

Aus Italien (1886), in which Strauss made his first cautious step away from the older abstract to the more modern poetic forms, was, according to tradition, largely influenced by the teaching of Alexander Ritter. But we need not attribute too much to this influence ; no doubt much of its strength came from the fact that it operated upon Strauss just when his musical imagination was losing some of its first metallic hardness and softening into something more purely emotional. We have already noted signs of this here and there in the later work of his first period, notably in the Piano Quartet. There seems, in fact, to have been a psychological change going on within him at this time, which probably had its origin in some subtle physiological change—some inteneration of the mental and bodily tissues

that brought with it a more nervous suscepti-
bility to feeling. The journey to Italy in the
spring of 1886 no doubt accelerated this process ; Italy disturbed and inspired the young
man's imagination as it has always done that
of sensitive Northerners—Goethe, Tchaikovski,
and Hugo Wolf, for example—when they have
visited it for the first time. In *Aus Italien*,
which was written immediately after his return
from the south, the pulse of Strauss's music is
perceptibly quickened and the temperature of it
heightened by the physical and mental sensa-
tions he had experienced in Italy *—more potent
influences in his development, we may be sure,
than all the arguments of Ritter. The emotional glow in the first and third movements
is as far above anything we meet with even
in the andante of the Piano Quartet as the
warmth of that is above the average temperature of the preceding works. A casual survey
of the first movement alone will show that here
everything is generated and controlled by
emotion. There is no music-making for music-

* Strauss is still peculiarly susceptible to sunlight.
He has told more than one friend that he cannot compose
in the winter; light and warmth are necessary before his
ideas will begin to flow.

RICHARD STRAUSS AS A BOY

making's sake, no mere strenuous turning of the wheel regardless of whether there is any corn being ground or not, as there was in much of the earlier vigorous but steely work; here the whole movement has its genesis in a personal emotion that has been sincerely felt and lived through. The music, too, has the broad deliberate onward sweep from its beginning to its end that is characteristic of so many of the later symphonic poems of Strauss; and although the composer here has wisely let the ideas determine the form, instead of attempting to fit them into a preconceived frame, the development is perfectly logical and the movement as a whole finely balanced and organic. In the third movement, again, depicting the feelings of the composer "By Sorrento's Strand," there is a sensitiveness to pure beauty—to the quality in music that gives the ear the same deep contented joy that the form and colour of beautiful flowers give to the eye—that marks a great advance upon anything of the kind that Strauss had attempted previously. Both this and the first movement, indeed, remain to this day among his most truly felt and exquisitely expressed works. We notice,

again, in this third movement, the beginning
of Strauss's many efforts at literary and pictorial characterization in music—though as
yet the tendency is kept within legitimate
bounds. The second movement is both the-
matically and emotionally interesting and is
well worked out. The finale, a representation
of Neapolitan popular life,* is the least satisfactory movement of the work. There is a
breezy vitality in a good deal of it, but as a
whole it does not hang together, the music
often bustling along in a way that is meant to
be vivacious but is merely fussy.

How much of the new warmth of feeling
and the more vitalized workmanship that
marked *Aus Italien* out from the earlier music
of Strauss was the outcome of his having a
poetic scheme to follow may be guessed from
the Violin Sonata composed in the following
year. Here, although at times the greater
depth of emotion and the superior technique
that Strauss had now acquired are clearly
evident, he is obviously not completely at his

* The first subject of the finale is the melody of
Denza's song "Funiculi, funiculà," which Strauss had
heard in Naples. He thought it was a Neapolitan folk-
song, and has so designated it in his score

ease in the more abstract sonata form. The
first movement is indeed remarkably rich,
strong, and well constructed ; the themes are
both striking in themselves and are treated
with much fertility of device, and the music
flows on in an almost unbroken current from
the first bar to the last. But the andante,
though there is a certain artificial charm in
some of the writing, notably in the arabesques
of the latter portion, has nothing like the depth
of meaning of either of the slow sections of
Aus Italien. To use a Coleridgian distinction,
it comes from the fancy rather than from the
imagination ; it is graceful and pleasant, but
the feeling is slightly self-conscious and rises
from no great depth. The finale is almost
wholly in Strauss's earlier manner—is, indeed,
rather more scrambling and inorganic than
most of his youthful finales. The Sonata
marks Strauss's final breach with the abstract
classical form ; he now recognized that what
he had to say was ill-fitted for this form, and
that it could only come to full expression in
the freer forms of poetic music.

This is not the place to attempt either a
summary of the history of programme music

or a detailed analysis of the æsthetic problems it involves.* A brief survey of the question is, however, necessary if we desire to apply a critical criterion to the later works of Strauss or to understand their significance in the history of modern music.

Roughly speaking, there are two kinds of musical idea ; the one is self-existent and self-sufficient, referring to nothing external to itself, and requiring no knowledge of anything but itself for the full understanding of it ; the other is prompted by some previous literary or pictorial concept and can only be fully understood in conjunction with this. At the one extreme stand musical ideas like those of the average fugue, or the " subjects " of a Mozart symphony ; at the other extreme stand ideas like those of a song or an opera. Midway between these two there lies a peculiar kind of musical idea that is not actually associated with words—as in the opera or the song—but

---

* The student who is interested in the subject will find a mass of historical information in Professor Niecks's recent large book, "Programme Music." For an attempt to solve the general æsthetic question perhaps I may be allowed to refer to a lengthy essay of my own in my "Musical Studies" (1905).

which, though it exists only in a purely instrumental form, really owes its being to the
desire to represent in music some other idea
non-musical in its origin. Types of this kind
of musical idea are seen in the tumultuous
string passages near the end of the " Leonora
No. 3 " overture, which symbolize the over-
whelming joy of Leonora and Florestan at the
happy ending to their sufferings ; in the
anguish-stricken opening phrases of Gluck's
" Iphigenia in Aulis " overture, which express the grief of Agamemnon ; in the
two melodies—one stern and forceful, the
other gentle and suppliant—that denote re-
spectively Coriolanus and the women in
Beethoven's " Coriolanus " overture ; in the
delicate flitting phrases that depict the fairies
or the braying phrase that depicts the ass in
Mendelssohn's " Midsummer Night's Dream "
overture ; in the thoughtful, mournful theme
which, in Wagner's " Faust " overture, por-
trays the old weary philosopher of Goethe's
poem ; in the phrases that suggest the flowing
water in the introduction to " The Rhinegold " ; in the phrases that suggest the whirring
of the spinning-wheels in " The Flying Dutch-

man " ; in the rhythms that suggest the galloping horse in Liszt's " Mazeppa " ; in the softly swaying harmonies that depict the rustling leaves in the " Waldweben " in " Siegfried " ; in the undulating melodies in which Bach often tries to suggest a river, or the broken phrases in which he tries to convey the idea of a man stumbling. We may conveniently call the first kind of music abstract and the second poetic, though we must always remember that a great deal of music that is ostensibly abstract is really poetic in its origin. There are many apparently abstract compositions which, like the " Revolutionary " Etude of Chopin, we know to have originated in a definite external stimulus ; and there must be a great many others which, though the composer has left us wholly without clue to their poetic intention, are certainly translations into tone of the impressions made by some book, or picture, or event, or aspect of nature. Probably, if the truth were known, two-thirds of the music of the past two hundred years belong rather to the category of poetic than to that of abstract music.

So far, however, we have been considering

only the basic ideas of a piece of music. These do not in themselves, of course, constitute a musical composition, but only the material out of which it is to be made ; and it is in this process of building fragments of musical material into a large and organic whole that the great point of contention arises between the abstract and the poetic musicians. We are face to face, in fact, with the great and eternal problem of form—the problem of making each bar of a composition lead so naturally and logically into the next that the whole tissue seems like a living organism, and of so balancing one part with another, and making each detail a necessary factor in the total effect, that the composition as a whole satisfies our sense of design as a perfect piece of architecture does. Composers have always instinctively striven after this architectural balance and proportion ; even the simplest song or dance shows it in its modulation, halfway through, into the key of the dominant and its return to the key of the tonic. In the development of modern musical form it was inevitable that for some time the composers should concentrate most of their attention on

what we may call the more external aspect
of " design " in music—on securing an obvious
and rather artificial balance, proportion, and
orderliness. We see the effect of this in the
conventional key-schemes and the sharply
separated " subjects " of the average eigh-
teenth-century symphony or sonata. Men
were voyaging on new seas and felt it unsafe
to venture out of sight of land ; they invented
subjects so pointedly different in style that
no one could help perceiving where one ended
and the other began ; and their simple schemes
of key-contrast and key-sequence threw no
strain on a sense of tonality that was as yet
almost in its infancy.

The obvious *lacunæ* in the symphonic structure of Mozart and Haydn were filled up by
Beethoven. He made each part of the music
grow organically out of and into the parts that
followed and preceded it ; he introduced a
wealth of new detail—melodic, harmonic,
rhythmic, and modulatory—yet built it all so
firmly and logically together that the total
effect is as of some great building of the utmost
harmony of design, in which practically every
stone that is used plays an indispensable part.

In every sphere of music the same ideal of form has to be striven after—logical continuity of tissue and perfect balance between the details and the mass.

But it is evident that abstract music can as a rule attain this ideal much more easily than poetic music. Music that is concerned with nothing but self-existent themes and their possibilities of metamorphosis has necessarily fewer difficulties in its way than poetic music, which has to pursue simultaneously two lines of development ; for it has to weave a connected musical tissue by the same process of evolution of new matter from old that goes on in abstract music, and at the same time it has to follow the lines laid down for it by its poetic basis. It is in the attempt to serve these two masters at once that so much poetic music comes to grief ; if the music pursues merely its own line of development it is apt to obscure or misinterpret the programme ; *

* I here use the term " programme " to cover every kind and every form of subject that music may attempt to express. In this sense the poem of a song or an opera is its " programme." Every student knows that there can be the same clashing between the words and the music of a song, for example, as between the programme and the music of a symphonic poem. On the one hand

E

while if the programme is followed with too
canine a fidelity the total design of the work
is likely to be imperfect—for literary form is
not musical form. The early nineteenth-century
experimenters in poetic music were soon made
to realize their dilemma. Berlioz never succeeded in discovering the new form that would
fit his new ideas. Liszt came nearer to the
ideal in his symphonic poems, in which the
poetic scheme was made to unfold within the
frame of a single movement, instead of the
three or four or five movements of the classical
symphony and the programme symphony of
Berlioz. But Liszt's powers of construction
were not equal to his powers of invention.
He could illustrate the details of a poetic subject expressively enough ; but almost all his
symphonic poems are weak in musical architecture. He never succeeded in striking the
proper balance between the claims of the
poetic scheme and the claims of the musical
tissue to develop in its own way ; and in his

Liszt, in his symphonic poems, often pursues the literary
idea at the expense of the purely musical development ; on
the other hand Schubert often writes pure music that
does violent injustice to the poem it is supposed to
illustrate.

anxiety that nothing of his programme shall remain unrevealed he often writes music that is a mere disorganized drifting from one literary point to another. He is a musical illustrator rather than a musical builder.

Poetic music, then, was for a long time in a dilemma. The method of Liszt and his more adventurous followers produced symphonic poems that were often admirably veracious in detail, but ill-knit and incoherent as a whole ; the timid neo-classicists, on the other hand, merely gave literary titles to pieces written in the conventional symphonic form. Yet the way out of the difficulty was perfectly plain. Since poetic music has to tell a story and at the same time to talk sound musical sense—for the ear will not tolerate, in the name of litera-ture, what it feels to be musical nonsense—obviously the proper course is to choose a programme the development of which will assist the purely musical evolution instead of placing obstacles in the way of it. The musical tissue must always be the paramount considera-tion. The poetic scheme to be illustrated should therefore, in the first place, be as con-cise and uncomplicated as possible, for, as music requires a large space for its own peculiar kind of development, no more than a hint from poetry is needed to start a lengthy musical discourse. Secondly, since much of what we call " development " in music consists of the re-presentation of the same thematic material in different forms—the ear finding one of its greatest pleasures in the recognition of variety in unity and unity in variety—it follows that the later episodes in the poetic scheme should bear such a relation to the earlier ones as can be logically expressed by metamorphoses of the earlier musical themes. The prelude to " Lohengrin " is so perfect because its underlying poetic idea—the angel hosts emerging from the distance, bearing the Grail nearer and nearer the spectator until its radiance blinds him, and then slowly receding into the distance again—is one that lends itself admirably to a typical musical device—that of starting a theme in the simplest terms, working up the possibilities latent in it to a huge climax, and then refining it away again to vanishing point. Here, of course, there is practically no incident ; and it is when the composer of poetic music comes to work upon a scheme that involves much incident that he realizes the difficulty of making his poetic and his musical development run on the same lines. It is this difficulty that Strauss has come nearer solving than any other composer of symphonic poems, partly because he has mostly been judicious in the selection of his poetic material, partly because of the extraordinary fertility of resource he has shown in the construction of the musical tissue of his work.

For Strauss is in reality one of the great musical builders. When belated partisans of the older schools call his music " formless " they simply mean that he builds in forms that transcend their own unprogressive conception of the meaning of the word. To them " form " means nothing more than sonata form ; the notion that there can be logic, unity, organic life in a composition put together on any lines but these is inconceivable to them. At bottom, indeed, the question is one not so much of form as of idea. All the music of the giants of the past expresses no more than a fragment of what music can and some day will express. With each new generation it must discover and reveal some new secret of the universe and

of man's heart ; and as the thing to be uttered
varies, the way of uttering it must vary also.
There is only one rational definition of good
" form " in music—that which expresses most
succinctly and most perfectly the state of soul
in which the idea originated ; and as moods
and ideas change, so must forms. The form
of the finale of the " Pathetic Symphony,"
for example, is perfect, because in no other
way could that particular sequence of emotions
be so poignantly and convincingly expressed.
As Mr. Bernard Shaw has recently pointed out,*
nothing more perfect in the way of " form "
could be imagined than the Preludes to " Lohengrin " and " Tristan " ; their evolution
from the first bar to the last is as inevitable
in itself and as beautifully rounded and complete as the slow passing of the hours in the
cycle from dawn to dawn. But for some
musicians, as has already been pointed out,
" form " means sonata form and nothing more ;
and they would crush all musical ideas into
this frame as Procrustes forced all his unhappy
captives to fit the same bed. Quite recently

* In "The Sanity of Art: an Exposure of the Current
Nonsense about Artists being Degenerate."

a London newspaper solemnly censured a new work in these terms : " The whole work is singularly lacking in contrapuntal interest, and depends solely for such effect as it achieves upon certain emotional impressions of harmony and colour." * It matters little to these good souls that the particular thing the composer wanted to say could only be said as he chose to say it, and that a display of counterpoint in the work might have been as ludicrously ineffective as a suit of medieval armour on a modern fencer. The only musical interest, for some worthy people, is contrapuntal interest ; and if a composer has ideas that do not call for contrapuntal jugglery—well, so much the worse for him. If a Whistler gets " certain emotional impressions of harmony and colour " from the play of a certain light on a fog-bank he must not try to convey his impressions to others and to make them see the beauty he saw in this vague vibration of colour ; he must paint us something tangible and substantial—a " Derby Day," for example, or a provincial Mayor in an aggressively

* I cull the quotation from Mr. William Wallace's recent book " The Threshold of Music," p. 98.

red robe. Any new treatment of a new
emotion must be shunned like the plague ;
the thing to be aimed at is " contrapuntal
interest."

The wild charge of " formlessness " that is
so often flung at Strauss comes, in fact, from
a failure to distinguish between form and
formalism. As the point is one of the utmost
importance to every student of modern music,
a little digression upon it will not be out of place.
The school that looks askance at Strauss takes
for its idol Brahms, who is described by his
more enthusiastic admirers as the last of the
great German masters, and acclaimed as " a
master of flawless form." Now any one who
looks at Brahms's symphonies, for example,
with eyes unclouded by tradition, can see that
his form is often far from flawless. He is less
a master of form than " form " is master of
him. He is like a man in whom etiquette
predominates over manners ; his symphonies
behave as they have been told rather than as
they feel. To say this is not to declare one-
self an anti-Brahmsian. One can admire to
the full all the profundity, the wisdom, the
humanity, the poetry of that great spirit, and

AS A STUDENT

yet contest his claim to be regarded as one of the kings of form. With Beethoven the form seems the inevitable outcome of the idea, as all first-rate, vitalized form should; with Brahms the ideas are plainly manufactured to fit the form. The supposed necessity for pacifying this traditional monster is visible on page after page. It cramps Brahms in the making of his themes, which often show the most evident signs of being selected mainly because they were easily "workable." This in itself is a mark of imperfect command of form; we should never smell the lamp in a work of art. Or, to vary the analogy, though a cathedral has to be begun with scaffolding, he is a clumsy builder who leaves pieces of the scaffolding still visible in the completed structure. A picture, as Sir Joshua Reynolds said, should give us the impression of being not only done well but done easily. In Brahms the labour, the calculation are often too apparent. We can overhear him muttering to himself, "Now I must have my theme in augmentation, now in diminution; now I must fit A into B— with what other end in view, indeed, did I make them both variants of the arpeggio of

the same chord ? * now I have reached my
double bar, and I must flounder about, more
or less helplessly, for a moment or two, till
I can get into my swing again "—and so on.
The whole movement, of course, is not made
up of cold calculations of this kind ; but there
are enough of them to prove that Brahms was
a slave to his form instead of being master of
it, and to make it impossible to place him
in the same category with Beethoven. Such
useless academic fumbling as that at the beginning of the repeat in the first movement of
the D major symphony, and in a good deal of
the first movement of the E minor, quite
destroys the vitality of the form for any one
who can think for himself instead of believing
blindly what the professors tell him. There
are too many patches of lead visible here and
there in the bronze statue for us to accept it
as flawless.

Strauss can afford to smile, then, at the
criticism that calls him " formless " because he
chooses to make his own forms to suit his own

* See, for example, the first subject and its supple-
mentary theme in the first movement of the D major
symphony.

ideas, instead of, like Brahms, making his ideas to fit some one else's form. And whatever harm he may unconsciously do to foolish young composers who try to imitate his methods, it is safe to say that it cannot surpass the harm that has already been done by the slavish adherence to the so-called classical forms. If the one influence is responsible for much wild and chaotic writing, the other must be blamed for a quite appalling amount of parrot-music that at its best is mere academic primness and at its worst is deadly boredom. The average academy-made composer, indeed, with his tiresome and futile attempts to make living music by the mechanical manipulation of a couple of arid " subjects," reminds us of nothing so much as some poor patient Hottentot rubbing two dry sticks together in the hope of getting a bit of fire. And when one sees how many capable and promising musicians have been stunted in their growth by this system of Chinese compression,* one wishes that somebody would write an exhaustive

* Busoni has some penetrating remarks on the subject, apropos partly of the finale to Brahms's first symphony, in his " Entwurf einer neuen Aesthetik der Tonkunst " (Trieste, 1907).

book on " Sonata Form, its Cause and Cure,"
and present a copy to every student who is in
danger of catching the disease.

Sonata form, in fact, was the special product
of a special order of musical ideas—the best
possible way of giving to those particular ideas
coherence, balance, and unity. But the ideas
—especially the musico-poetic ideas—of this
generation are not those of the eighteenth
or early nineteenth century, and the old
methods of building ideas up into large designs
are no longer wholly applicable ; coherence,
balance, and unity must still be sought, but
in different ways. It is Strauss's great virtue
that he has shown how this can be done. He
is as solicitous about " form " as the most
hide-bound pedant could be ; he himself has
said, in reply to a question that was a little
indiscreet, " I always have form before my
eyes in composing." The defects in his later
orchestral works, and they are regrettably
many, are not at all of form but of conception—
they come from that lack of balance in his
disposition that makes it impossible for him
to keep the cruder and more freakish side of
his nature under ; but even when he is spoiling

RICHARD STRAUSS AS A STUDENT

a fine picture by inserting in it details that set our teeth on edge by their inappropriateness or their inanity, he always weaves his threads together, the cotton with the silk, in masterly fashion. In *Ein Heldenleben*, for example, those of us who would willingly go out of the hall, if we could, while the " Adversaries " are sniggering and snarling and grunting, are bound to admire the skill and the power with which he later on builds the chief "Adversary"theme into the main musical tissue. And as for breadth and scope of design, the orchestral works from *Tod und Verklärung* onward show a grasp of musical architecture and an audacity of mental span that can be paralleled, in the nineteenth century, in the work only of Beethoven and of Wagner. Beside the power that builds up such an edifice as *Zarathustra* or *Ein Heldenleben*, the Brahmsian faculty for going through the conventional forms of scholastic jugglery with two or three fragments of carefully selected material does not seem so wonderful that we should go into rhapsodies over it.

As we have seen, Strauss made the transition from abstract to poetic music very cautiously.

Aus Italien shows him carefully feeling his
way from the one to the other ; though he is
working upon a programme * he still adheres
in the main, like Berlioz, to the older symphonic
form. The work is in four movements, each
bearing a title—(1) " In the Campagna "
(*andante*) ; (2) " Among the Ruins of Rome,"
with the sub-title " Fantastic pictures of
vanished splendour ; feelings of melancholy
and sorrow in the midst of the sunny present "
(*allegro molto con brio*) ; (3) " By Sorrento's
Strand " (*andantino*) ; (4) " Scenes of Popular

* There is not space in the present volume for a discussion of the æsthetic justification of programme music.
I have attempted this in the essay in " Musical Studies "
to which I have already referred. But comparatively
few people nowadays would hold to the old opinion that
programme music is the accursed thing. The question
used to be regarded as settled by Beethoven's remark
about his Pastoral Symphony being " mehr Ausdruck als
Malerei." No one troubles about that now, except to
note that the symphony itself flatly contradicts the theory.
It is, curiously enough, Wagner who is now put up as the
bulwark against the insidious invader. His theory that
representative music is only fully comprehensible when
there is a stage action to elucidate it, and that it is impossible to keep the programme of an orchestral work
in one's head while following the music, has received
more reverence than it deserves. I have elsewhere shown
that Wagner's theory was simply the expression of his
own bias towards stage work. If he could not visualize for

Life in Naples " (*allegro molto*). All the while there can be seen the contest in the young composer between the traditions of his past and the first stirrings of his future style. The work is formal and free by turns ; it is neither pure poetic mood-painting nor pure abstract design, but a compromise or a fluctuation between the two. Strauss had not yet mastered the art of framing his programme in such a way that no clashing shall result between the poetic scheme and the musical structure, the two evolving at the same rate along parallel

himself the protagonists of a symphonic poem like *Ein Heldenleben*, that is no reason why other people, who *can* visualize them, should give up doing so. And Wagner's own work is an emphatic contradiction of his theory. The " Flying Dutchman " and " Tannhäuser " overtures and the " Lohengrin " prelude require us, if we are to understand them fully, to keep in our minds certain sequences of external events without any help from the stage. His orchestral picture of Siegfried's Rhine-Journey again, in the " Gotterdämmerung," is programme music pure and simple. The mind has to associate certain characters with certain themes, and imagine certain changes of scenery and action, just as it has to do, for instance, in Tchaikovski's " Romeo and Juliet " overture. But the vast general question cannot be discussed here ; and in the text of the present chapter it is assumed that the reader accepts the broad principle of programme music just as he does the symphony, the opera, or the oratorio.

lines. *Macbeth* (1886-7) shows a marked advance in this respect ; it is really a superior
work, from the point of view of form, to *Don
Juan*, which was composed in 1888. In *Don
Juan* Strauss meets for the first time with one
of the main difficulties of the symphonic poem
—that of combining a mass of disparate
material, partly psychological and partly concerned with the narration of external events,
in one satisfactory picture. The finest pages
of *Don Juan* are those in which the nature of
the programme allows the musician to give
free play to his power of pure musical development—as in the first portrait of Don Juan
himself, in the duet between him and the
Countess, in the portrait of Anna, and in the
tumultuous final section commencing with the
theme in the four horns. The unsatisfactory
portions of the work are those—such as the
brief suggestion of the country maiden *—that
are dragged in willy-nilly for a moment without forming any essential part of the tissue
as a whole, and the carnival scene, where the

* It is obviously impossible to find space in this little
volume for an analysis of each of Strauss's symphonic
poems. Many excellent detailed " guides " to them,
however, can be obtained.

sudden changing of the kaleidoscope, together with something not quite convincing in the music itself, strikes rather a jarring note. In *Don Juan*, in fact, magnificent as the work as a whole is, the canvas is a little too crowded and the various parts of the picture are not balanced finely enough. *Macbeth* avoids these faults by living throughout, as it were, in the one medium. It is all psychology and no action. If Strauss were to write a *Macbeth* to-day he would probably not be content with the soul alone of the character ; he would make him pass through a series of definite adventures, and the score would be half penetrating psychology and half exasperating realism. His taste was purer in 1887 ; and in many ways *Macbeth*, though it has never been so popular as the other early works of Strauss, is a model both in its instinctively right choice of material and in its musical *facture*. There are, it is true, a good many startling effects, but they are all justified by the subject. Strauss makes no attempt whatever to cover the whole ground of Shakespeare's drama ; no other character is introduced but Lady Macbeth— and she is really kept in the background of

F

the picture—and absolutely nothing "happens," not even the murder of the king. The whole drama is enacted in the soul of Macbeth; apart from the comparatively few bars that depict his wife, the score is entirely concerned with the internal conflict of the three main elements of his character—his ambitious pride, his irresolution, and his love for Lady Macbeth. There is nothing here that is not pure "stuff for music," as Wagner would have said. The musical texture of the work is extraordinarily strong and well-wrought; already the young man of twenty-two makes Liszt seem like an amateur in comparison. For the first time in the history of the symphonic poem, in fact, a musical brain of the best kind, endlessly fertile in ideas and with a masterly technique, is cultivating the form. The score, youthful as it is, already shows the rich polyphonic structure that is characteristic of Strauss, and beside which the homophonic, lyrical style of Liszt seems decidedly thin.

In *Don Juan*, while the superb vitality of the work as a whole and the exquisite beauty of episodes like the love-song of Anna and the duet with the Countess are what give it its main interest, there is some excellent work-manship. When the nature of the poetic programme allows the musician to take the bit into his own mouth, as it were, and run a long course unchecked, we get some pages of the finest development that the history of the symphonic poem can show—the music unfolding itself, bar by bar, with as perfect continuity and consistency as if it had nothing but itself to consider, while at the same time it keeps adding fresh points to our knowledge of the psychology of the character it is portraying. No other composer equals Strauss in this power of writing long stretches of music that interests us in and for itself, at the same time that every line and colour in it seems to express some new trait of the individual who is being sketched ; perhaps the finest example of the kind is the long introductory section of *Ein Heldenleben*. In *Don Juan* Strauss's purely musical powers touch a higher point than they had reached in any of the earlier work. *Macbeth* is characteristic and veracious rather than beautiful, as indeed was inevitable from the nature of the subject ; in *Don Juan* the flame of beauty burns brightly and passionately almost throughout. But we notice here, for the first time in Strauss's work, the tendency to overburden music with extraneous and inassimilable literary concepts. Most people will agree that, besides its own purely intensive world of expression, music has some jurisdiction over parts of territories that belong to literature or to painting. No one but the most short-sighted of æstheticians will deny that besides expressing the inmost heart of man, music can depict or suggest a vast number of external things. It is useless to protest that were it not for the programme we should never know that such and such a sequence of notes was meant to represent, say, a sunrise or the flowing of water. Every schoolboy knows that; all we contend for is, that given the clue, given the literary or pictorial image, music can greatly deepen and heighten it and so add enormously to our pleasure. The fire music in " The Valkyrie " would not of itself make a man who knew nothing of the story shout " Fire " the first time he heard it; but when the stage shows us fire and the characters are talking about fire, the leaping and flickering and crackling of the orchestra make it so much more vivid for us. In the same way the idea of Siegfried's sword is greatly intensified by the flashing trumpet theme that accompanies it, and the idea of the flowing Rhine is intensified by the surging and undulating chords of the intro-duction to the " Rhinegold." All this is per-fectly legitimate ; it is in fact only a further application of a principle that is to be seen everywhere in vocal music ; no one, for in-stance, without a knowledge of the words of the song, would guess that the pianoforte accompaniment in Schubert's " Gretchen am Spinnrade " was intended to suggest a spinning-wheel ; but when he knows the subject of the poem, the whirring phrases in the piano help materially to bring the poet's and the musician's picture before his eyes.

Strauss has been more daring and more ingenious than any musician but Wagner in his suggestions of this kind ; and most people would agree that his representations of the dying shudder of Don Juan and the dying sigh of Don Quixote, for example, are not mere intellectual eccentricities, but really poignant emotional effects. But it is one thing to ex-

tend the scope of musical speech in this legitimate way, and quite another to make a bogus
extension of it by merely tacking a literary label
on to a handful of notes that cannot possibly
be made to mean what the label says they
mean ;   and Strauss is unfortunately rather
given to deluding himself in this manner.   The
Rhine music really suggests flowing water ;
the fire music really suggests flickering fire ;
the sword motive really suggests something
flashing and piercing ;   and the " swan "
motive in " Lohengrin," though of course it
does not suggest a swan—which it is not meant
to do—really suggests the ethereal purity and
calm of Montsalvat, of which the swan is only
-the visible symbol.   But when Strauss writes
this sequence of notes—

and tells us that it is meant to signify a feeling
of satiety in Don Juan's heart, we are bound
to tell him that it does nothing of the kind—
there is no congruity, as there is in the other
cases, between the literary label and the

RICHARD STRAUSS' COUNTRY HOUSE AT MARQUARDTSTEIN, WITH THE ZUGSPITZE

musical phrase. And when later on, by combining this " satiety " motive with that of Anna—

he tries to tell us that while the lady loves Don Juan, the hero has grown a little tired of the lady, we feel that Strauss is striving to make music perform a purely intellectual task for which it is quite unfitted. So again with the theme of " disgust " in *Also sprach Zarathustra,* that blares out in the trombones at the end of the section descriptive of " Delights and Passions "—

In the first place this no more suggests disgust than it does the toothache ; and when at a later stage he brings in the theme in diminution—

and asks us to see in this the partly convalescent Zarathustra making sport of his previous depression of spirits,* we can only say that we are unable to oblige him.   All we are conscious of is that a sequence of notes that had very little meaning to begin with is now being made unnecessarily ugly and ridiculous.

In *Don Juan,* then, we can see Strauss setting his foot for the first time on the false path that has led him into so many marshes and quicksands.   Still the mischief so far is not

* These themes are not labelled, of course, in the scores ; but every one knows that the titles given to them represent Strauss's intentions.   The minute analyses of his symphonic poems that are now issued in Germany are obviously based on information supplied by him.

very great. Nor is there any error of taste or judgment of this kind to distress us in his next orchestral work, *Tod und Verklärung* (1889). As regards the union of pure form with unalloyed purity of material this is perhaps the most perfect thing he has done. The architectural plan of *Ein Heldenleben* is vaster and grander; but there are one or two crude deformities in the building that sadly mar the total effect. In *Tod und Verklärung* Strauss has come nearer than anywhere else to that perfect fusion of matter and style that is the ideal of all the arts. The poetic scheme is free from any matter that is not essentially musical,* and it develops in such a way as to afford the musician the amplest facilities for development of his own special kind. The tissue of the work is woven with admirable closeness and continuity, and at the same time with great economy of means. The old material is constantly being presented in new forms; even a merely rhythmic fragment

* It should be remembered that the poem by Alexander Ritter that is prefixed to the score was written after, not before, the music; Strauss worked upon a skeleton scheme of his own. Some German critics hold that Ritter's poem is not true to the music at every point.

like the " death " motive with which the
symphonic poem opens becomes charged, in
the sequel, with all kinds of significances,
poetic and musical. In *Tod und Verklärung*
we have a quite Beethovenian unity and
breadth of conception. The work is one and
indivisible; it gives the first sign of that breadth
of span, that ability to hold all the detail of
one's scheme in the hollow of one's hand and
see the finished structure as it will ultimately
appear, that is the characteristic only of the
greatest builders in art—what Pater has called
" that architectural conception of work which
foresees the end in the beginning and never
loses sight of it, and in every part is conscious
of all the rest, till the last sentence does but,
with undiminished vigour, unfold and justify
the first."

In *Till Eulenspiegel* (1894–5) the form is
again developed with consummate cleverness ;
the eloquent and witty transformations of the
original themes interest us both by their purely
musical quality and by the vividness with
which they suggest this or that aspect of the
hero of the poem. It has been frequently
pointed out that Strauss's form always has

a peculiar appositeness to his subject. The adventures of Till Eulenspiegel are best told in rondo form ; the form of a theme with a series of variations is the one most suited to *Don Quixote ;* and there are similar reasons, rooted in the nature of the scenes or the moods that have to be painted, for the forms of all the other orchestral works from *Macbeth* to the *Symphonia Domestica.* In *Till Eulenspiegel* the thematic development is carried on with an ease and a copiousness of invention that are a constant delight to the musician ; while the whole work glows with good spirits and rings with kindly laughter. Strauss's comedy here sounds a more generally agreeable note than anywhere else, except in parts of *Don Quixote.* After the latter work his comic sense acquires an unpleasantly acid taste ; in *Ein Heldenleben,* for example, he has lost the art of tolerant laughter, and can only grin and grimace unpleasantly and rather savagely at the follies of mankind. In *Till Eulenspiegel,* in fact, all the components of his nature are still held in an approximate balance. After this, while he deepens notably in some respects, touches some sublime heights of feeling, and

sounds some extraordinary depths, the general
balance of his work is upset. The impish side
of his temperament gets more and more out of
his control, and he is increasingly inclined
to overcrowd the programmes of his symphonic
poems with literary or pictorial ideas that
are generally beyond the power of music to
express.

This latter tendency is most evident in
Also sprach Zarathustra (1894–5), in a sense
the most thoughtful of his works, but nevertheless the one which will perhaps fade the
soonest. The conception as a whole is a
monumental one, and the work contains
some of the noblest music that Strauss has
written. But music cannot properly cover
some of the ground laid out in the programme ;
and there are one or two sections where, in
spite of the titanic power with which Strauss
tries to overcome his difficulties, the musical
tissue of the work wears very thin. At times
we miss altogether the splendid continuity
of weaving of the earlier symphonic poems ;
there are places where the composer checks
the stream of his musical development altogether in order to play off one thematic

fragment against another in a way that may enforce the literary or philosophical point he is driving at, but which certainly does not make organic music. The work is an illustration of one of the dangers to which, as we have already seen, the modern symphonic poem is peculiarly exposed—that of working upon a literary plan too full of episodes for the music to get a fair field for continuous development of its own. These defects will probably be enough to make *Also sprach Zarathustra* age more rapidly than any other orchestral work of Strauss. Just as a chain is no stronger than its weakest link, so a work of art is no stronger than the weakest page in it ; and the pages in *Zarathustra* that are musically weak are numerous enough to interfere seriously with our appreciation of the rest. In the great bulk of the score the workmanship is fully as strong as that of any other of his works up to this time ; there is the usual breadth of view in the total design and the usual fertility of device in the use of the details of the material. It is astonishing, indeed, how near he comes, time after time, to overcoming the difficulties inherent in the nature of what is perhaps

the most difficult subject ever set by a musician;
he is a Titan in chains, but still a Titan.

Here and there in *Zarathustra* we can detect
traces of the freakish element that is so strong
in Strauss's character, and that has come more
and more to the front since *Till Eulenspiegel.*
The serious nature of the subject, however,
and the elevated mood in which the composer
undoubtedly approached it, allow this element
to give no more than an occasional hint of its
existence. In his two next big works, however, *Don Quixote* (1897) and *Ein Heldenleben*
(1898), it breaks bounds and goes a long way
towards spoiling two of the finest scores of the
nineteenth century. By this time Strauss's
technical facility and his command over his
own ideas had become quite remarkable ;
there was nothing he could not do with his
material. On the purely formal side, both
Don Quixote and *Ein Heldenleben* are perfectly
masterly ; there seems to be no limit to his
inventivenesss or to his power of presenting his
themes in always new and always thoroughly
interesting forms ; and he writes the most
complicated polyphony with astounding ease.
We need not lay too much stress on the famous

passage in *Ein Heldenleben* where some twenty-four themes from his earlier works are combined with each other and with themes from *Ein Heldenleben* itself in a most amazing fabric of sound. No doubt much of this can be called counterpoint only by courtesy; as a well-known conductor said to his orchestra, *apropos* of the passage, you can combine any number of themes together, if you are not too particular how it all sounds. But the extraordinary thing is that a great deal of this apparently haphazard interweaving of themes really does sound well; and the music as a whole exhales a sentiment of melancholy that is of course just the psychological effect that Strauss was here aiming at. Still, remarkable as is this *tour de force*, it remains little more than a *tour de force*, and we must not dwell too much on it. But in a score of other places in *Don Quixote* and *Ein Heldenleben* the polyphony has all, or more than, the cleverness of the passage just referred to, without its sense of pose, of consciously setting itself difficulties merely in order to overcome them.

There are the same strength and the same

inexhaustible variety of invention in the thematic development of the two works. In *Don Quixote* the modern variation form may be said to have received its apotheosis. The method inaugurated by Wagner of denoting a character by a theme, and expressing the changes in the character by variations of the theme, is here carried to its furthest possibilities; every psychological change in Don Quixote is expressed with infallible certainty in a variation of the original theme. In *Ein Heldenleben* Strauss's power of securing variety by changes in the thematic material, that at the same time interest the ear for their own sakes and elucidate the programme, is seen at its very finest. In largeness of general conception, in the fine sense of form that controls the vast design, and in the skill with which all the themes are made, in this or that metamorphosis, to play organic parts in the development of the work,* it stands at the head of all the symphonic poems we know.

* The reader may be recommended to study these theme-transformations for himself, either from the score alone or with the help of a " guide." He should notice how even such a small fragment as the figure of four semiquavers in the third bar of the introduction is put to the most varied and most expressive uses later on.

RICHARD STRAUSS' COUNTRY HOUSE AT MARQUARDTSTEIN

But unfortunately at this time Strauss had lost something of his earlier balance of soul and his earlier fineness of taste. There had grown up in him a deep love of the grotesque for its own sake ; and music happens to be the art in which the grotesque most jars upon us and most quickly wearies us. In *Don Quixote*, perhaps, Strauss's descents into a kind of humour that is not far from farce are not so exasperating, because of the fundamentally comic nature of much of the subject. We could well do without such things as the extraordinary imitation of the bleating of the flock of sheep ; but since we are given them, and they are so audaciously clever, the best thing is not to mount the high horse in dudgeon, but to see the situation from the composer's point of view and to laugh with him. But though the atmosphere of *Don Quixote* will permit us, if we are not too strait-laced, to take this tolerant view of what, when all is said, is still a blot on a great work of art, the atmosphere of *Ein Heldenleben* will permit nothing of the kind. There the feeling is so much more tense that any lapse into the grotesque is doubly irritating. The " Adver-

G

saries " section, though considered by itself it has a certain humour of an essentially poor kind, strikes one, coming in where it does, as merely a piece of laborious stupidity, unworthy of a man of Strauss's genius. The " battle " section, again, though we must needs admire the intellectual energy and the technical skill of it, is a blatant and hideous piece of work. There must be a flaw, one thinks, in the mind of a man who can deliberately spoil a great and beautiful artistic conception by inserting such monstrosities as these in it. After *Ein Heldenleben* it looked as if some subtle poison had entered into Strauss's art, and one began to have fears for his future. The *Symphonia Domestica* (1903) did not dispel these fears. The work made a sensation at the time, partly because the simplicity of the subject—papa, mamma, and baby—brought the programme, at any rate, within the scope of the intelligence of the average man. People who were puzzled almost to the point of insanity by *Zarathustra* and its "Uebermenschen," and its "Genesende," and all the rest of that queer fauna, could recognize at once when the baby was squealing in its bath or the lullaby was being sung over it ;

and they had a kindly fellow-feeling for the terrible musician who now seemed to be even such a one as themselves. But the work, as music, was mostly unsatisfactory to musicians. It has its great and uplifted moments, such as the love scene, and there is considerable beauty in a good deal of the music that is written round the child. But the texture as a whole is less interesting than in any other of Strauss's works, the short and snappy thematic fragments out of which he builds it contrasting badly with the great sweeping themes of the earlier symphonic poems ; the instrumental colour is grossly overdone ; the polyphony is often coarse and sprawling ; and the realistic effects in the score are at once so atrociously ugly and so pitiably foolish that one listens to them with regret that a composer of genius should ever have fallen so low. Since the *Symphonia Domestica* Strauss has not given the world any opportunity of judging whether he has recovered his earlier balance as an orchestral writer, or whether he has lost it irrevocably. He has brought out no purely orchestral work since 1903, with the exception of five Military Marches (1906 and 1907), which are quite negligible in a survey of his evolution. They merely say next to nothing in a very highly coloured way.

In the foregoing rapid sketch of his orchestral works, attention has been mostly concentrated on his development on the formal side. It is here that, as has already been pointed out, Strauss has given a new life and new meaning to the symphonic poem. He has put at once more brains, more music, and more technique into it than any of his predecessors or contemporaries. He has really added a new chapter to the history of musical form—a chapter one does not yet find in the text-books merely because the text-books are all so intent upon the dead that they have no eyes for the living form. At its best his orchestral music is as finely and firmly woven as the best of purely abstract music could be. He has done for programme music what Wagner did for opera—taken up the stray threads that earlier men had been fumbling with more or less ineffectively, added a great deal of new stuff of his own, and woven it all into a fabric of undreamt-of strength of texture and richness of colour. At present we cannot imagine any further extension of the symphonic poem, as we cannot imagine any further extension of the Wagnerian music-drama. No doubt both will come some day ; but the present generation is not likely to see the symphonic poem filled with a more exuberant life, planned on a larger scale, or worked out with a keener or surer sense of design than it is in Strauss.

Perhaps these are questions for musicians rather than for the general public, which probably thinks little and cares little about design in music. The public goes to music for expression ; it may not know that the C minor symphony or " Tristan " is an almost faultlessly constructed piece of architecture, but it does know that there is something in these works that moves it profoundly. Can Strauss move the world in the same way ? One of the commonest and cheapest of the current disparagements of him is that he is an intellectual rather than an emotional man—that his music comes, in the stock phrase, from the head instead of the heart. There is no disputing about tastes, of course ; but the idea that Strauss is not an emotional musician is incomprehensible to many of us. His work, indeed, seems filled with a greater flood of feeling, and with more varieties of feeling, than that of any other living musician. He has greatly enlarged the boundaries of musical expression ; the blend of humour and pathos in *Don Quixote,* in particular, is something wholly new in music. It is not emotion that he lacks, but that balance of all the faculties that one sees in the very greatest artists. There is something excessive, *déréglé,* in his nature—and, one is bound to say, something small, something of that petty passion for flouting the Philistine that is the mark of a mind not so free from the limitations of the Philistine as it imagines itself to be. The ugly, nervous laughter at his critics in the " Adversaries " section of *Ein Heldenleben* is not merely a blot on the work ; it gives one a startled sense of the strain of weakness there is in Strauss, both as artist and as philosopher. No doubt the virulence and the ignorance of his critics have done much to embitter him ; but to let them agitate him to the extent of making him spoil a great masterpiece in order to fling some of their own mud back in their faces is to come down to their level. No harmoniously built artist, we may be sure, would have lost his head like this. Beethoven would have set his teeth, dismissed his opponents from his mind, and gone on writing for himself, sustained by the proud consciousness of his superiority. Wagner satirizes his critics in " Die Meistersinger," but not feverishly or unkindly, and not in a way that mars the general texture of his work ; the artist in him was too strong to be overcome by any recollection of the petty annoyances of daily life. Strauss lacks this serenity of soul, this power to withdraw wholly into himself ; and when a man uses his music to gibe venomously at people because they have gibed at him, we feel that he is not the complete, self-poised artist one would like him to be. The earlier works, as far as *Till Eulenspiegel,* have a mental balance that the later ones all lack in some way or other, and for which no advance in grandeur of general conception or profundity of feeling can compensate us. A new orchestral work that should have the rounded unity and uninterruptedly high seriousness of *Tod und Verklärung* together with the larger sweep and subtler emotion of *Don Quixote* and *Ein Heldenleben* would indeed be something unique in modern music. Will Strauss ever give us this ? Will he, as he grows older, master the cruder side of him, or will it continue to force itself, as it has been doing since 1895, further and further into the foreground, spoiling his best work in proportion as it becomes visible?

CHAPTER IV

STRAUSS has written over a hundred songs, but a careful study of them gives one the impression that he is not a born song writer, and that comparatively few of his Lieder have much chance of survival. This verdict may surprise those who have often felt, when some fine song of his has been sung in the interval between two of his orchestral works, that this is a Strauss they could more readily take to their hearts than the composer of *Ein Helden-leben* or *Don Quixote*. Critics, too, on occasions like this, have been known to lament that Strauss did not cultivate further his tender and charming lyrical vein. But the songs that have made this effect have been some half-dozen of the very best of the hundred ; and it is too hastily assumed that all, or the majority, of the rest are of the same high quality. As a matter of fact, one very small volume will contain all the Lieder of Strauss that are worth living with day by day. Nowhere, in truth, does he show to such poor advantage on the whole as here. He has written some good songs, and one or two exquisite songs, but also a number that are commonplace, or dull, or pretentiously empty, or stupid, or downright ugly. Only those who have conscientiously worked through them all a few times, desirous of seeing good in them wherever it is to be seen, can realize the woeful waste of time and labour that the majority of them represent.

How some of them came to be written can no doubt be easily explained. A composer has many " calls " to composition, and perhaps the most seductive, siren-like call of all is that of the publisher jingling what Stevenson called the clinking, minted quids. When a musician can get forty or fifty pounds for a single lyric, as Strauss now can, the temptation to believe in the theory of his own plenary inspiration must be irresistible. A number of his songs may be frankly written off as not music but merchandise. Others are failures

RICHARD STRAUSS AND HIS FATHER
Reproduced from a photograph in the possession of Mr. Alfred Kalisch

from various reasons. Some of them, such as *Die Frauen sind oft fromm und still* (op. 21, No. 5), are tiresomely didactic ; others, such as *Wozu noch Mädchen* (op. 19, No. 1), *Ach weh mir* (op. 21, No. 4), *Fur fünfzehn Pfennig* (op. 36, No. 2), *Hat gesagt* (op. 36, No. 3), *Herr Lenz* (op. 37, No. 5), *Bruder Liederlich* (op. 41, No. 4), *Von den sieben Zechbrüdern* (op. 47, No. 5), *Ach was Kummer* (op. 49, No. 8), and *Junggesellenschwur* (op. 49, No. 6), aim at a primitive kind of facetiousness that is bad enough in any art, but intolerable in music. One or two of these songs, in spite of their occasional cleverness, give us unpleasant hints of how far along the road to inanity a Teutonic genius can travel when he is bent on being funny. Strauss is highly commended by some of the German critics for setting the most modern German poets to music, such as Liliencron, Dehmel, Henckell, Bierbaum, Mackay, and Morgenstern, in contrast with Hugo Wolf, who associated himself only with dead writers, like Goethe, Heine, Geibel, Heyse, Mörike, and Eichendorff, and, though he was very friendly with Detlev von Liliencron, set no poem of his to music. Strauss is supposed

to have founded a new order of song, the
" social lyric," the expression of the life of our
own day. As, however, he has chosen to set
most of these modern poems to quite un-
interesting music, it is difficult to be very
grateful to him ; and though the words of
" Who is Sylvia ? " are shockingly old, most
of us would prefer Schubert's setting of them
to all the turbid cascades of notes that Strauss
has poured over the words of " modern " poets
like Bierbaum and Mackay. There is no
particular credit in setting the poems of living
writers if the poems are unsuitable for music,
as many of those which Strauss has composed
undoubtedly are.

His questionable taste in poetry rather
implies that he is not a born musical lyrist,
for the true modern song writer, like Hugo
Wolf, is prevented from choosing bad poetic
material by an instinctive sense that it cannot
be converted into good music. Strauss, in
fact, decidedly lacks that power of harmonious
and balanced structure on a small scale that
is the first essential of the song writer. He
has, as we have seen, a remarkable gift for
musical architecture on a large scale, but the

smaller the ground on which he has to work the more visibly is he hampered. A song by Wolf can be seen at once to be woven in a single piece ; one broad conception dominates it all, and is instinctively felt to be implicit in all the changing details as they unfold themselves. Many of Strauss's most ambitious songs are absolutely formless, with no more organization than a jellyfish ; the music simply wanders on from one line to another without reason and without connection. Play through things like *Anbetung* (op. 36, No. 4), *Mein Herz ist stumm* (op. 19, No. 6), or *Am Ufer* (op. 41, No. 3), and you will have merely a queer sense of having drifted aimlessly through one key after another and from one part of the scale to another, such vague emotions as have been stirred now and then being quite unrelated to each other, and the song as a whole suggesting no general emotional mood whatever. In songs like this Strauss creates no vision in us because he has had none himself to begin with ; he has started off without any central idea or feeling, and just does the best he can with each line as it appears—living, as it were, from hand to mouth until the thing

is over. In a communication to Friedrich
von Hausegger, in 1903, he told the world his
way of writing songs. For some time, he says,
he will have no impulse to compose at all.
Then one evening he will be turning the leaves
of a volume of poetry; a poem will strike his
eye, he reads it through, it agrees with the
mood he is in, and at once the appropriate
music is instinctively fitted to it. He is in
a musical frame of mind, and all he wants is
the right poetic vessel into which to pour his
ideas. If good luck throws this in his way,
a satisfactory song results. But often, he
says, the poem that presents itself is not the
right one ; then he has to bend his musical
mood to fit it the best way he can ; he works
laboriously and without the right kind of
enthusiasm at it. The song, in fact, is made,
not born. This confession explains all his
failures as a lyrist. Wolf always started from
the poem ; he absorbed himself so utterly in
it that for the time being he really *lived* it,
and the music with which it spontaneously
clothed itself was simply the equivalent in
tone of the emotion that had penetrated the
poet when he wrote the words. Strauss

begins from the other end. He sits down to read with a vague musical feeling in him calling for expression. If now he chances to find a poem that perfectly fits this musical feeling, he reaches, though from the reverse direction, precisely the point that Wolf reached. But if the vague musical mood has to accommodate itself, as best it can, to a poem not thoroughly propitious to it, it is evident that there can be no particular felicity of detail, and, above all, none of that sense of completeness, the sense of gradual and irresistible evolution from the first bar to the last, that makes Wolf's songs so satisfactory from the point of view of form.

To this unfortunate lack of agreement between the poet and the musician we owe a number of Strauss's least admirable songs. As he feels nothing in particular he can express nothing in particular, so he relies on a display of pumped-up excitement that he hopes may be mistaken for genuine passion. In songs like *Mein Auge* (op. 37, No. 4), *Auf ein Kind* (op. 47, No. 1), and *Frühlingsfeier* (op. 56, No. 5), one would think, from the deluge of black notes that rains upon the page, that something of the utmost significance was being said ; but when we look at the song critically we see that it all amounts to very little or nothing at all. There is a superfluity of this pretentious emptiness in Strauss's songs —pounds upon pounds of notes from which we can hardly squeeze a half-ounce of feeling or even of meaning. And he often experiments in his songs in audacities from which even he would shrink in his orchestral works. Occasionally these tricks are entertaining, as in the charming *Ich schwebe* (op. 48, No. 2), where the faintly clashing progressions have an agreeable piquancy of their own. But in many of the songs he seems absolutely to lose himself in jungles of his own planting ; * there are some pages—as for example, in *Himmelsboten* (op. 32, No. 5), *Glückes genug* (op. 37, No. 1), and *Die Ulme zu Hirschau* (op. 43,

* At a certain point in *Wenn* (op. 31, No. 2), Strauss adds a facetious footnote to the effect that singers in the nineteenth century are recommended to transpose the song, from this point onwards, a semitone lower, so that it may end in the key in which it began. This particular modulation, however, is quite harmless. Whatever the nineteenth century may think of it, the twentieth century will probably solve the problem in the simplest possible way—by deciding that the song is not good enough to be worth singing at all.

No. 3)—that are sheer melodic and harmonic
nonsense. People who take a malicious delight
in dwelling upon the uglinesses in Strauss's
orchestral works should spend a day or two
with his songs ; they would find sins enough
against not only beauty but against sanity
to provide them with texts for a year's ser-
mons.

Strauss has not grown as a song writer in
the way that he has grown as an orchestral
writer, gradually evolving a unique personal
style of his own. There is a long road between
Ein Heldenleben and *Aus Italien*, and a bigger
figure at the end of it than at the beginning ;
but in his songs with pianoforte accompaniment there is not very much difference between
the Strauss of 1886 and the Strauss of 1906.
The best songs of 1906 are not much better
than the best of 1886 ; the bad ones of 1886
are no worse than the worst of 1906 ; and good
and bad still jostle each other cheerfully in
the same opus number. Yet Strauss has grown
in the sense that he has shaken off the influence
of Liszt that was so pronounced in his earlier
songs. In songs like *Sehnsucht* (op. 32, No. 2),
O wärst du mein (op. 26, No. 2), and *Ruhe,*

H

meine Seele (op. 27, No. 1), the manner is quite
Lisztian—a way of working conscientiously
from one line to another without any thought
of unity of total effect, of padding out a rather
inexpressive vocal theme with a multitude of
notes in the piano, and of dragging a simple
poem out to a quite inordinate musical length.
Liszt's songs often suffer from this kind of
elephantiasis ; the delicate tissues of a little
poem swell in the most alarmingly dropsical
way under the treatment of the musician.   He
cannot set *Die todte Nachtigall*, for instance,
to music, without digging a grave for the
poor little bird big enough for a turkey.
There is something of this over-elaboration
in Strauss's earlier style ; it can be seen in
such songs as *Hoffen und wieder verzagen*
(op. 19, No. 5), and *Mein Herz ist stumm*
(op. 19, No. 6), and others, as well as in the
three already mentioned.

   Few of his songs have the concision and
the simplicity—the air of not employing one
note too many—that makes Wolf's work so
admirable.   The simple, indeed, is rather out
of Strauss's reach as a rule ; when he attempts
it, as in *Du meines Herzens Krönelein* (op. 21,

No. 2), *All mein Gedanken* (op. 21, No. 1), *Muttertändelei* (op. 43, No. 2), *Einkehr* (op. 47, No. 4), *Des Dichters Abendgang* (op. 47, No. 2), *Wer lieben will* (op. 49, No. 7), *Mit deinen blauen Augen* (op. 56, No. 4), he is generally either dull and charmless, or too self-consciously pretty. Yet every now and then he has, by a miracle, pared down his expansive style to the limits of the lyric, and then we get the songs of his that we may be sure will live. At first the emotion, genuine though it is, is a little solid and beefy, as in the popular *Zueignung* (op. 10, No. 1), and *Allerseelen* (op. 10, No. 8). Then it grows more refined, and in songs like *Seitdem dein Aug* (op. 17, No. 1), *Serenade* (op. 17, No. 2), *Morgen* (op. 27, No. 4), *Traum durch die Dämmerung* (op. 29, No. 1), *Schlagende Herzen* (op. 29, No. 2), *Nachtgang* (op. 29, No. 3), *Ich trage meine Minne* (op. 32, No. 1), *Meinem Kinde* (op. 37, No. 3), *Befreit* (op. 39, No. 4), *Die sieben Siegel* (op. 46, No. 3), *Winterweihe* (op. 48, No. 4), *Ich schwebe* (op. 48, No. 2), *Blindenklage* (op. 56, No. 2), and some others, his feeling is at its purest and his technique at its best, the songs being mostly cast in one piece throughout. Now and then he achieves something wholly original, as in the powerful *Lied des Steinklopfers* (op. 49, No. 4), and *Der Arbeitsmann* (op. 39, No. 3), where the social humanism of the emotion is very thrilling.

Like Wolf, Strauss throws much of the burden of expression in his songs on to the accompaniment, though he rarely shows Wolf's art of blending the piano part and the voice part in one indivisible whole. With Strauss not only is the voice part sometimes overshadowed by the accompaniment, but the latter is often over-elaborated till it becomes a mere hindrance instead of a help to the feeling. His style, in truth, is not a piano style. He keeps up a higher average level of interest in his songs with orchestral accompaniment, where he has the kind of colour he can make most suggestive and the breadth of canvas that suits him. Even here he can be merely noisily pretentious and fussy, as in *Nächtlicher Gang* (op. 44, No. 2) ; but such powerful and fluent pieces of work as the *Notturno* (op. 44, No. 1), *Hymnus* (op. 33, No. 3), and *Pilgers Morgenlied* (op. 33, No. 4), give us the sensation, which so many of the pianoforte songs do not,

that here we are in the company of the greater
Strauss. Of the whole of his large output of
songs, probably not more than twenty or
twenty-five can rank as perfect or approxi-
mately perfect successes.

Space permits only the briefest reference to
Strauss's choral works. The early *Wandrers
Sturmlied* (1884-6) showed him to have a
thorough command of choral polyphony ; he
obviously delights in the opportunities the
medium affords him for stupendous effects of
vocal tone. In its poetic feeling, its vigour,
and its ease of workmanship, it is one of the
finest pieces of choral and orchestral writing
of the nineteenth century. The orchestra is
again combined with the voices in the *Taillefer*
(1903), in which there are solo voices also, and
in the *Bardengesang* (1906). The former,
though a trifle unequal, is a most spirited piece
of work. Neither here nor in the *Bardengesang* is there much attempt at subtlety in the
choral writing ; the effects achieved are
mostly those of sheer depth and massiveness.
The *Bardengesang* is magnificently barbaric,
though it slightly tries one's gravity as the
chorus thunders out the names of the tribes—

Ha, ye Cheruseans! Ye Chattees! Ye Marsians!
Ye Semnonians!
Ye Brukterians! Ye Warnians! Ye Gothonians!
Ye Lewovians!
Ye Reudinians! Ye Hermundurians! Ye Naris-
kians! Ye Quadees!
Ye Trevirians! Ye Nervians! Ye Nehmetians! Ye
Wangtonians!

and so on.

Of the unaccompanied choruses of Strauss the most striking are the two anthems of opus 34, written in sixteen parts. The second is the more beautiful of the two, but both are masterly pieces of work. The three male-voice choruses of opus 45 and the two of opus 42 are also for the most part brilliant and expressive. The *Soldatenlied* for male voices, published without opus number, is merely a boisterous *jeu d'esprit*, no doubt greatly relished by the German student in his more festive moments.

This chapter seems the most appropriate place also in which to refer to the recitation music to " Enoch Arden " (op. 38), written at the request of Strauss's actor-friend, Possart. The union of the speaking voice with the pianoforte is at the best a detestable one.

Strauss's highly expressive music, however, is well worth studying on its own account. It shows, among other things, to what varied uses he could put a small leading motive or two.

CHAPTER V

BOTH Strauss's first opera, *Guntram,** and his second, *Feuersnot*, are neglected now in Germany, and there are many who think that *Salome*, in spite of the magnificence of much of the music, will before long share the same fate. There are special reasons in each case for this. They lie mostly in the nature of the subjects and the libretti; Strauss's operatic music is quite as remarkable as his orchestral music, and in the opera house, as in the concert room, he has, in spite of his faults, no equal among contemporary composers for depth and range of expression.

The libretto of *Salome* is based on Frau

* Strauss calls *Guntram* and *Salome* "Musikdramas" and *Feuersnot* a "Singgedicht." We may conveniently call them all three operas, declining to follow the Teutonic mind in its mania for giving different names to what is essentially the same thing.

Hedwig Lachmann's German translation of Oscar Wilde's play ; Strauss has done nothing more than abridge this for his own purposes. The libretto of *Guntram*, however, is entirely his own work ; that of *Feuersnot* is by Ernst von Wolzogen, but the idea of it was given him by Strauss, and it is probable that the musician had something to do with the composition of the poem.

The story of *Guntram* was suggested to Strauss by a newspaper article on certain secret societies that existed in Austria in the Middle Ages, whose objects were partly artistic, partly religious and ethical. Guntram is a young knight who belongs to one of these societies, the members of which call themselves "Die Streiter der Liebe" ("The Champions of Love ") ; their office is to soften the hearts of men by their songs, and so to lead mankind to universal brotherhood through love. Guntram has set out upon this work, accompanied by an older member of the order, Friedhold * ; he is to intercede with the tyrant Duke Robert

* Friedhold is said by Dr. Arthur Seidl to be meant to suggest Alexander Ritter. He sees certain resemblances between the doctrines of *Guntram* and those of Ritter's opera "Wem die Krone? "

for his sorely oppressed subjects. The scene
opens in a woodland glade, where Guntram
is sharing his bread and fruit with a number
of these poor people. Hunger and misery
stalk through the ravaged land ; a rebellion,
into which the people were goaded by their
sufferings, has just been mercilessly put down.
The Duke's wife, Freihild—" the Mother of
the Poor "—who at one time did what she
could to alleviate their lot, has now, they tell
Guntram, been forbidden by her husband to
help them. The poor people leave the scene,
followed by Friedhold, and in a long mono-
logue Guntram meditates upon the beauty
and innocence of nature and of his own childhood, and upon the suffering brought into
this idyllic world by the cruel passions of men.
He springs to his feet, and calls in fervent
words upon the Saviour to help him to touch
the heart of the Duke by his song and to bring
peace to the oppressed poor. He is about to
leave when a woman rushes in distractedly,
intending to drown herself in the lake at the
back of the glade. This proves to be Freihild,
who has been reduced to despair by the re-
fusal of her hated husband to allow her to

show sympathy with his subjects. Guntram holds her back in spite of her entreaties; she believes him to be merely one of the ordinary Minnesingers, whom she holds in small esteem. He learns her name by the cries of "Freihild" that come from the old Duke, her father, who has been searching for her in the wood with his retainers. He asks Guntram to name his reward for rescuing his daughter; Guntram begs for the pardon of a number of rebels who have been captured by Robert and are threatened with dire punishment. The request is granted, though much against the will of Robert; and the Act closes with every one making for the court of the Duke, where a feast is to be held in honour of the return of Freihild and the conquest of the rebels.

The opening of the second Act shows these festivities in full swing. After the praises of Robert have been sung by the servile Minnesingers, Guntram rises, seizes his harp, and delivers a long and impassioned eulogy of the beauties of peace and freedom (the "Friedenserzählung"). His eloquence moves every one except the brutal Robert; even some of the vassals begin to murmur against their

ruler. At last Guntram denounces Robert to
his face ; the latter attacks him with his
sword, but Guntram thrusts first, and Robert
falls dead. All are horror-struck. The old
Duke at first regards the crime as a pre-
meditated one, the object being to seize
Robert's kingdom. He gravely and sadly
asks Guntram to complete his work by slaying
him also ; the minstrel, however, is lost in
amazement at his own act, and merely stares
into space, unconscious of what is going on
around him. In time the old Duke recovers
his self-control and his command over the
previously wavering vassals ; at his orders
they arrest Guntram, imprison him, and then
march away to wreak new vengeance on the
rebels. Only Freihild and the court Fool are
left ; the latter is a sympathetic soul who feels
for the poor people, and is at the same time
deeply but humbly in love with his tender
mistress. In Freihild's breast a strong love
has grown up for Guntram, who has delivered
her from a hated spouse and the land from a
cruel tyrant. She conceives the plan of flee-
ing with him, and prevails upon the Fool to
secure his escape. This the Fool does, though

he mournfully recognizes that it means he will never see her again ; he promises to drug the drink of the gaolers and take Freihild into the prison cell.

The third Act takes place in a dungeon ; outside can be heard the chant of the monks who watch round the body of Robert. Guntram, a prey to remorse, is haunted by the spectre of the man he has murdered. He is roused from his painful reverie by the entrance of Freihild, who makes a passionate confession of the love his noble song has aroused in her bosom, and implores him to fly with her. To her astonishment and despair he announces his intention of leaving her for ever. Just as he runs to the door, Friedhold enters ; he has been sent by the Brotherhood of the " Streiter der Liebe " to bid Guntram to appear before them, and make his atonement for having slain a man and so transgressed the laws of the order, which are founded wholly on love. Guntram refuses to go, and then explains everything to Friedhold and Freihild. He has indeed committed a crime. But this did not consist in the mere fact of killing the Duke. The act itself was good ; it was the motive of the act that was bad, and the real motive, he has found on examination of his own heart, was earthly love for Freihild. For this no organization of men can punish him ; his punishment can come only from himself—he must renounce Freihild for ever. Previously he had believed in the outward laws that bind men ; now, illuminated by sad experience, he knows that no one but himself has jurisdiction over the spiritual part of him :—

> Eine einzige Stunde
> Hat mich erleuchtet,
> Doch jetzt bin einsam,
> Allein mit mir selbst!
> Meinen Leid hilft einzig nur
> Meines Herzens Drang;
> Meine Schuld sühnt nur
> Die Busse meiner Wahl;
> Mein Leben bestimmt
> Meines Geistes Gesetz;
> Mein Gott spricht
> Durch mich selbst nur zu mir.

The Fool enters with the news that the old Duke has been killed, and the whole land rejoices that Freihild is now its ruler. Guntram bids her assume the office and fill it for the good of the poor and the suffering. Incapable of speaking, she kneels down and kisses his hand; in the deepest emotion he bids her farewell and goes forth alone.

The theme of the opera will be recognized as a blend of Wagner and Nietzsche—a little of the " Uebermensch " of the philosopher coming in to complete.the musician's favourite doctrines of " renunciation " and " redemption by love." No doubt its Wagnerian tinge is one of the causes of the failure of *Guntram* to keep the stage; the world is growing a little weary of all these good but rather tiresome people who are continually renouncing, or being redeemed, or insisting on redeeming some one else; it finds it a little hard to bear even in Wagner, and will not stand much of it from any other musician. The occasional slowness of the action, the long stretches of rather nebulous philosophizing, and also, it is said, the difficulty of finding tenors capable of performing the part of Guntram, are other reasons why the opera has been shelved. It is a pity that it should be so, for *Guntram* is a remarkable piece of work. It is quite true that the musical style, like the poetic, shows many traces of Wagner's influence. The scene in the Court, where Guntram sings to

the assembly, reminds us of " Tannhäuser,"
and there are other situations that suggest
" Parsifal." There is something of the " Waldweben " in Guntram's poetic reverie in the
first Act ; there are suggestions now and then
of " Lohengrin " ; and one of the love themes
is so plainly taken from " Tristan " that one
wonders how Strauss himself could help
noticing the close similarity. There are, too,
a few pages in the score where the writing is
thick and lustreless, and one or two places
where the effort to be " characteristic "—to
" paint " in music—has caused Strauss to
write music that is merely forced and ugly, as
in the case of the theme typifying the rigid
laws of the Brotherhood,* which is almost
as violently illogical as some of the writing in
the songs. But the bulk of the score touches
a high plane of beauty, and curiously enough,
in spite of the occasional Wagnerism of the
music, the style throughout gives one the
impression of being personal to Strauss. The
high seriousness of the work and the spirit
of humanism that breathes from it are exceed-

* See, for example, the statement of it at the beginning
of the prelude to the third Act.

ingly impressive ; *Guntram* alone, with its
ardour of love, and above all, the tenderness
of its sympathies for humanity, is sufficient
to refute the superficial notion that Strauss is
merely a clever intellectualist playing at being
a musician. Some depth of thought and very
considerable depth of feeling have gone to the
making of the work. The character drawing
is a little inexpert here and there. Guntram
and Freihild and the moaning, lamenting
people are clearly and convincingly limned ;
the others are not characterized in the music
with anything like the same veracity. The
musical tissue is, like all Strauss's work, endlessly rich in ideas ; there is a grandeur of
manner at times, a long-sustained energy of
invention, that is to be met with elsewhere
in no other operas but those of Wagner. And
Strauss shows in *Guntram* the same power as
in his orchestral works of devising themes
that are both expressive in themselves and
fertile in possibilities of development ; the
various metamorphoses of the leading motives
and their interplay with each other are carried
out in a masterly way. Altogether *Guntram*
is a great work, the many merits of which will

I

perhaps some day restore it to the stage from which it is now most unjustly banished.

Some eight or nine years elapsed between the composition of *Guntram* and that of *Feuersnot*. In the interval Strauss had written *Till Eulenspiegel*, *Also sprach Zarathustra*, *Don Quixote* and *Ein Heldenleben*, so that by 1900 his individual style was fully made, and the score of *Feuersnot* is wholly his own, not a trace of Wagner's manner being visible.

He got the idea of the opera from an old saga of the Netherlands, entitled " Das erloschene Feuer zu Audenaerde." This tells of a certain young man who loved a maiden, who, however, was cold and contemptuous towards him. At last, pretending to relax her severity, she told him that if he would place himself in a large basket on the following night she would draw it and him up to her chamber. The young man was in the basket punctually at midnight ; but the false maiden only drew him half-way up the wall of the house and left him suspended there, to suffer in the morning the gibes of all the townspeople. When he was released, burning with rage, he went to an old magician in a neighbouring wood and asked him to revenge him upon the maiden. The magician instantly extinguished every light and every fire in the town. When the distressed citizens at length assembled to discuss what should be done, the magician attended the meeting, disguised as a venerable burgher. After exacting from them all a promise that they would follow his advice to the uttermost, he told them that the failure of the fire was due to the unkind treatment of the young man by the maiden, and that as a penance she must appear in the market unclothed. Each of the burghers was to bring a candle to the scene. The reluctant maiden was made to remove her clothing, whereupon a flame darted out from her back. From this all the candles of the town were lighted, each burgher conscientiously refusing to take a light from the candle of his neighbour, but going direct to the parent flame itself.

In this form, of course, the story was quite unsuitable to the stage. Strauss and Wolzogen, however, with only a few alterations, made it quite workable and decidedly much more charming than it is in its original shape.

The action of the opera—which, by the way,
is in one Act only—takes place in Munich,
on midsummer eve in the " fabelhafte Unzeit "
(legendary No-Time). The scene is laid in
the Sentlingergasse. The children are going
from house to house, in accordance with an
old custom, begging wood for their fires.
From the Burgermeister, Ortolf Sentlinger,
they get a large basketful of wood, while his
beautiful young daughter, Diemut, and her
three companions give them sweetmeats and
dainties. All their thumping at the door of
the house on the opposite side of the street
produces for a long time no effect. The
neighbours give varied descriptions, favourable and unfavourable, of the inhabitant,
from which it appears that he is a young man,
Kunrad by name, who lives in complete
solitariness, and of whom little is known. At
length he appears at the door of the house,
looking absorbed and puzzled at the noise;
he has been immersed in study, and finds it
hard at first to comprehend what is going
on in the outer world. When he finally
understands that it is midsummer eve, and
that the jovial fires are being lit by the chil-

dren, a revulsion of feeling comes over him; he will give up dreaming, and live and enjoy like the rest. He tells the children to take as much of the wood of his house as they can as his contribution to their festival, and sets them the example by tearing the rotten old window shutters to pieces. Meanwhile, he has been gazing with ardent admiration at Diemut; and he suddenly signalizes his return to humanity by kissing her on the mouth, much to her annoyance and to the scandal of the burghers.

The crowd leaves the stage, going towards the gate where the fire is to be kindled. Diemut, nursing her wrong and planning vengeance, is seated at the balcony of her father's house. Kunrad, in the street below, confesses his love to her. She appears to yield to his request to be admitted to her chamber, and points to the basket that has contained the wood given by her father to the children. He enters it; she draws it up part of the way, and then pretends that her strength is unequal to pulling it any further. Down below, her three girl companions have been watching the progress of the plan. They

laughingly call the citizens to the spot, and
Kunrad is at last aware of how he has been
duped. In vehement tones he calls on his
magician friend to help him by extinguishing
all the lights and fires in the town. This
immediately happens. Every one now hastens
to the house ; the citizens are angry, the children are scared ; the only contented souls
are a number of loving young couples, who
softly express their cordial satisfaction with
the sudden darkening of the town. By this
time Kunrad has swung himself on to the
balcony of the house, whence he laughs at
the crowd below. Then he harangues them
at length ; he tells them that in his old house
there once dwelt a great master, one Reichardt,
who did the town great good and brought
great honour upon it, for which he received
nothing but envy and hatred. He himself
has been called to continue the work of the
old master, but for this he needs the sustain-
ing light of womanly love. The extinguishing of the fires has been a punishment for
Diemut's scornful conduct ; and they will
not be relit until she has done appropriate
penance for her crime. Diemut, who has

secretly loved Kunrad all the time, now appears on the balcony and draws him into her chamber. Down below the crowd comments on the matter and waits for the sign that the penance has been completed and that Diemut has atoned for her previous " gottverlassene Sprödigkeit." The moon has now disappeared, and the town is in total darkness. Only the tenderest tones of the orchestra, and of a harp, glockenspiel, and harmonium behind the scenes, are heard. Then a faint glimmer of light is seen through the windows of Diemut's room ; the love music in the orchestra grows more and more passionate, and as it reaches its climax all the fires and lights in the town simultaneously blaze out again, amid the joyous cries of the citizens. The voices of Kunrad and Diemut are heard for a moment, behind the scenes, blending in a cry of love, and as the curtain goes down the children are seen dancing gaily, and the citizens looking up at Diemut's window and congratulating the Burgermeister, her father.

The score of *Feuersnot* is an extraordinary blend of simplicity and profundity ; the utmost strength and daring of technique and the most gorgeous wealth of orchestral colouring go hand in hand with the most exquisite sweetness and naïveté. Passages like the love scene, or that in which Kunrad declares his love for Diemut, touch as high a point of passionate beauty as Strauss has ever reached, except perhaps here and there in *Salome*. On the other hand, nothing could surpass, for pure, simple, heart-easing charm, the melodies in which he has delineated the more homely features of the story, such as the merry-making of the children and the colloquies of the townspeople. He uses several old Munich folk-songs, but, delightful as they are, none of them is equal to his own melodies in the folk-song manner—the lovely choruses of the children, for example, and the melody sung by Diemut near the beginning of the opera, where she distributes the sweetmeats among the little ones. The whole work, in fact, with its glow and vivacity, gives one the impression of having been a pure delight to the composer. There are comparatively few instances in it of that tendency to false or exaggerated characterization that mars so much of Strauss's later work ; as a whole the opera is notably lucid and restrained, in spite of its passion and its constant high spirits. The reason of its failure to keep the stage must be sought elsewhere than in the music. Perhaps the story does not commend itself to all tastes ; and it must be confessed that once or twice, especially when the populace is waiting for the light to appear in Diemut's chamber, the language is of a freedom that has no parallel in opera libretti. To many people, no doubt, the tincture in the score of the " Ueberbrettl " spirit, of which Wolzogen is the accredited representative in Germany, is not altogether agreeable ; though one would think that people have only to take the fundamentally naïve atmosphere of the work as it is to enjoy it all thoroughly.

Perhaps, again, the satirical tendency of some parts of the opera tells against it. Strauss has used it as a mouthpiece for his own feeling of soreness at the comparative neglect that had been his lot in his own native city of Munich. It had been similarly ungrateful to Wagner in the sixties, during the patronage of him by King Ludwig ; the intrigues against

him were at one time sufficiently strong to
drive him from the town. The old master
Reichardt who once inhabited Kunrad's house,
and who had been so ungratefully treated
by the burghers, is of course, Richard Wagner ;
as Kunrad speaks of his power over the spirits
the orchestra softly gives out the Valhalla
motive from the " Rhinegold." The allusion
is driven home still more patently later on,
when, in a few neat lines, there are plays
upon the names of both Wagner and Strauss,
as well as that of the librettist, Wolzogen :—

> Sein (i.e. Meister Reichardt's) Wagen kam allzu
> gewagt Euch vor,
> Da triebt Ihr den Wagner aus dem Thor.
> Den bösen Feind, den triebt Ihr nit aus,
> Der stellt sich Euch immer aufs Neue zum Strauss
> Wohl zogen mannige wackere Leut',
> Die ein wagendes Wirken freut,
> Fern aus dem Reich in dem Isargau,
> Zu wipfelfreudigem Nesterbau.

And that Strauss regards himself as the
successor of Wagner is made quite clear to
us by the fact that Kunrad inhabits Meister
Richardt's old house, and has received from
the old master some excellent advice as to
how to do his work and how to treat the

public when it praises or blames him. Later on the burghers say the same thing :—

> Erwählt ward er vom Alten
> Des hohen Amts zu walten.
> Ihr doch in eurem Unverstand
> Habt keiner nix gespürt, noch gespannt.
> Weil er vom Ort gebürtig war,
> Meint Ihr, war's net weit mit ihm her.

All this is quite true and very delightful, but the fun and the satire are much more effective in one's own room, among one's friends, than in the theatre. Satire ages soon, because the thing satirized passes out of general memory ; and the difficulty of recalling it is all the greater when the appeal has to be made to so intellectually diverse a crowd as a theatre audience.

Salome, like *Feuersnot*, is in one Act, running on without a break for nearly two hours. Like the earlier opera, again, it has no overture. The scene is the terrace in Herod's palace ; at the back is a cistern in which John the Baptist is confined. Narraboth, a young Syrian captain, and some soldiers, are on guard. Narraboth commences, after three bars for the orchestra, with a eulogy of the

beauty of the young princess, Salome, who
is in the banqueting hall, feasting with Herod,
her mother Herodias, and the Court. While
a page tries to dissuade him from his mad
passion for the princess, which presages evil
for him, the voice of John is heard from the
cistern, prophesying the coming of a mightier
One than he. Further conversation goes on
among the soldiers ; then Salome leaves the
banqueting hall and comes upon the terrace.
She has been unable to endure any longer
the amorous glances that Herod, her mother's
husband, has been casting at her, and has come
to the terrace for the coolness of the air. The
Baptist's voice is again heard. Salome is
arrested by it ; she inquires who he is, and
learns that it is the prophet of whom Herod
and Herodias are both afraid. Her curiosity
is aroused, and she finally so works upon the
love of Narraboth for her that he disobeys
the strict orders of Herod and has the Baptist
brought up from the cistern. He immediately
breaks out into denunciations of Herodias and
her sins. Salome conceives a mad passion
for him ; it gradually overmasters her, and
she gives vent to her wild longing for him in

language of the utmost abandonment, the recurring burden of which is, " I will kiss thy mouth, Jokanaan." Narraboth, distracted by love for Salome and fear of the vengeance of Herod, slays himself at her feet ; but neither this nor the exhortations of John can restore her to sanity.

At last he curses her and goes down again into the cistern. Herod, Herodias, and the Court come upon the scene. He is excited with wine, nervous, superstitious, and ill at ease, imagining ill omens to be all around him. He is again pursuing Salome when the voice of John is once more heard from the cistern. Herod declines to yield to Herodias's desire that the prophet shall be given up to the Jews, for he is " a holy man who has seen God." This leads to a dispute among the Jews who are present as to the sanctity of John, and as to whether any one since Elias has seen God—a grotesque and comic musical *tour de force*. John's further denunciations of Herodias anger her, and when Salome finally dances in response to the entreaties of Herod, who promises her any reward she may ask, even unto the half of his kingdom,

Herodias supports her daughter in her demand
for the head of John. Herod, sobered now,
for a long time tries to dissuade Salome from
this ; at last he is compelled to give the ring
of death to a soldier, who takes it to the
executioner. Salome listens in silence at the
wall of the cistern, until the great black arm
of the executioner rises, bearing the head of
John on a silver shield. All are horrified
except Herodias, who smiles, and Salome,
who seizes the head and delivers a long and
passionate address to it. He would not let
her kiss his lips, she says ; now she will kiss
them. " If thou hadst seen me thou wouldst
have loved me. I am athirst for thy beauty ;
I am hungry for thy body, and neither wine
nor fruit can appease my desire. . . ." Herod's
terror deepens ; he bids the slaves put out
the torches, and the stage is in darkness.
Salome's mad rhapsody still goes on, and at
last becomes unendurable by the terrified
Herod. A ray of moonlight illumines her ;
Herod calls out wildly, " Kill that woman,"
and the soldiers crush her beneath their
shields.

It is easy enough to talk enthusiastically of

Salome, or to disparage it ; but to look at it critically is a very difficult matter, so full is it of new and bewildering things. Some parts of it, such as the scene between Salome and John, and the final scene of Salome with the head, are recognized at once to be entrancingly beautiful ; it is remarkable, indeed, what depth of real feeling Strauss gives, by his music, to Wilde's cold, mechanical, enamelled lines, and the wax flowers of his imagery. And even where the music is not beautiful, but merely a tissue of cunning *tours de force* of characterization and stage suggestion, it sweeps us off our feet. But whether this latter kind of thing will keep its interest for us is another question, that only time can answer. The dazzling cleverness and the inexhaustible wealth of colour in the score, the marvellous ingenuity with which every terrible detail of the scene or the psychology of the actors is brought home to us by the orchestra—these things are literally the world's wonder at present. But already we can see that there is much in the opera that is sheer ugliness, and the style has a good deal of that cold perversity that is so repellent in all Strauss's later work. Difficulties are created simply for the pleasure of overcoming, or trying to overcome, them ; the straight road to the desired end is ostentatiously avoided simply because it is straight. And although it is almost impossible for any man yet to make up his mind finally about *Salome*, it is quite clear that it marks no improvement on *Don Quixote* and *Ein Heldenleben* and the *Symphonia Domestica* in the one point in which improvement would have been most welcome. While Strauss's genius certainly develops in strength and beauty in one direction, it as certainly shows degeneration in another. We get from the opera the same impression as from the later orchestral works, that Strauss is incapable now of making a large picture sane and harmonious throughout ; somewhere or other he must spoil it by extravagance and perversity and foolishness. He can do every clever and astounding thing that a musician could do ; what he apparently cannot or will not do now is to write twenty continuous pages that shall be wholly beautiful and unmarred by bravado or by folly.

It is premature, of course, to attempt to appraise the final value of a musician who is still only in his forty-fourth year, and who may, therefore, in the normal course of things, be expected to have many years of activity yet before him. The difficulty is all the greater in the case of a man like Strauss, each one of whose works seems to inhabit a new mental world and to create a new musical style. Nevertheless, so much of his music has been long familiar to us that it is possible to look at it critically and even historically. One thing is certain, that he has put into music a greater energy, a greater stress of feeling and a greater weight of thinking, than any other composer of the day. There is not one of his larger works since *Aus Italien* that is not different in outlook and in idiom from all the rest. Like Wagner and Wolf, he is Protean ; his sympathies seem to have no restrictions, and his idiom varies with almost every work he writes. No musician, indeed, has ever repeated himself less, in so large an output, than Strauss has done. His style is marked by no constantly recurring mannerisms, such as we meet with in the works of

K

other men—the phrase-repetitions of Tchaikovski, for example, the arpeggio-born melodies of Brahms, the two-bar limp of Grieg,
or the slavery of Debussy to certain favourite
harmonic combinations. Strauss's melodies
and harmonies are endlessly new. There is
a " Strauss manner " in orchestration that
can be imitated because the factors of it—
the instruments—are the same for every one ;
but there is no " Strauss manner " in melody
or harmony that can be imitated, for these
are never wholly the same in two successive
works. There is only one characteristic of
his melodies that can be detached by analysis,
and this is not imitable in a way that could
deceive any one who knows the originals ;
his melodic line is notable for the great sweep
of its curve, the heights and depths it com-
passes within a bar or two. This freedom
of line is, indeed, one of the reasons for the
impression of superabundant energy that so
many of Strauss's melodies give us.

Harmonically he has apparently not inno-
vated so much as Debussy, but then he is
always master of his harmonies, can always
see and think his way through them, which

Debussy frequently cannot. Harmony is the one matter in which the artist is always ahead of his public ; we have only to remember how strange "Tristan," or even some parts of "Tannhäuser," sounded to us at a first hearing to recognize that a great deal of Strauss's apparent harmonic anarchism will look like ordered simplicity itself in another twenty years. Even now it is amusing to turn up some of the criticisms of works like *Tod und Verklärung* upon their first performance in this country, and to see how chaotic many people thought this music, which now seems as lucid as a page of Mozart. There are, it is true, several passages in his work, more especially in the songs, to which we cannot imagine human ears ever being reconciled ; they are as demonstrably nonsensical as a paragraph of print that has been dropped by the type-setter and recklessly put together again by the first man who picked it up. And there are other passages where the conclusion seems obvious that Strauss does not hear tonal combinations quite as we do. The unpleasant sequence of sevenths in *Ein Heldenleben*, for example—if it is not a mere piece of

freakishness, which hardly seems likely—
probably sounds differently in Strauss's ear
from what it does in ours. It must be remembered, too, that his style is often highly
polyphonic; and many a sequence in his
orchestral works that seems obscure to the
man in the street is perfectly intelligible if
listened to with the polyphonic as well as the
harmonic ear.

In orchestration he is an acknowledged
master. It is quite true that he is sometimes
excessively noisy, and that he often falls a
victim to the modern mania for using a pot of
paint where a mere brushful would do equally
well or better. There are plenty of passages
in his later works where the means employed,
the number of notes written, and the amount
of blowing or scraping or thumping done by
the players in the orchestra, are out of all
proportion to the effect obtained; as he himself has happily put it in his edition of Berlioz's
treatise on instrumentation—where he warns
young composers against the follies of over-
colouring which he constantly commits himself—it is not worth while sending out an
army corps to catch a skirmisher. But on the

whole his orchestration is the most daring and successful thing of its kind since Berlioz's. It has not the almost infallible certainty of the scoring of men like Wagner and Elgar, who love sheer beauty of orchestral colour too much to play any tricks with it ; but in spite of its many uglinesses and frequent miscalculations it is a marvellous storehouse of new and wonderful effects of tone-colour. What will be the ultimate result of some of his innovations it is hard to say. His appetite for increased wood-wind, horns, and brass, for new instruments, such as the heckelphone that is used in *Salome*, and for older instruments, such as the saxophone, that are not part of the ordinary orchestra, seems to grow with what it feeds on. To many of us a lot of this colour, which at best only thickens the picture instead of illuminating it, appears wholly superfluous ; the score of the *Symphonia Domestica*, for example, would sound just as well with a third of the notes and several of the players omitted. But it is hopeless to appeal to the reason of composers in this matter ; and the only satisfaction, the only hope of salvation for music and for our

ears, is that the material consideration of
expense will always do something at least to
check this hæmorrhage of notes. Composers
will some day have to choose between writing
orchestral works, with scores of instruments,
for merely mental performance, and writing
works that are within the financial possibilities
of the average concert society or opera house.

This excess of orchestration in Strauss's
later works is only part of a general tendency
to excess that has become increasingly evident
during the last few years. On all sides—in
his choice of subjects as well as in his treatment of them, in his harmonic system and his
orchestral technique—he shows a disposition
to an extravagance that will ultimately do
his art no good. What the cause of this may
be it is hard to say. Some of it may be due
to physical and mental overstrain, the result
of a more strenuous life than any man who
wishes to keep his brain and nervous system
at their best has any right to live ; Strauss's
youthful balance and athletic self-control
may have been partly destroyed. Some of
it, on the other hand, may come from a
deliberate intention to stagger humanity.

If, as seems likely, Strauss has been embittered by some of the opposition he has had to contend with, we can only regret that it should be so. But the fact remains that something unpleasant has come into his art during the past few years. When we think of the high-minded seriousness and the self-mastery of works like *Tod und Verklärung* and *Guntram*, and then of the grimaces and twitchings and mad laughter that deface so much of the later work, it is impossible to feel that Strauss's genius is developing as a harmonious whole.

Yet with all his present faults he remains by far the most commanding figure in contemporary music. In the preceding pages I have tried to indicate his real significance in history ; he has carried programme music to apparently its ultimate limit by applying the Wagner-Liszt system of theme-transformation with an audacity and a brilliance of which they never dreamt, and by turning upon this kind of music all the force of an energetic and teeming brain and a marvellous technique. He has already enriched music with more new ideas than any musician since Wagner. He has made music realistic, not only in the coarse sense

of material imitation, but in the high sense
that with him musical character drawing has
become extraordinarily poignant and veracious.
Such humour and such pathos as those of
Don Quixote, for example, represent a quite
new phase of musical psychology. He has
got away from the wigs and tights and the
stage apparatus of Wagner, and by his music
alone paints for us the kind of men and women
we see around us day by day. But unfortunately his indiscriminate worship of reality,
together with an unexampled cleverness of
technique, has led him to attempt to express
too much in music. He is apt to become too
pictorial, too external, too crudely suggestive.
And the very vehemence of these attempts
will bring about all the sooner the general
reaction that is bound to come in European
music, a reversion to simpler methods and
more purely emotional moods. Perhaps he
himself, as he grows older and wiser, may lead
this reaction. At present his greatest admirers cannot help admitting mournfully that for
some years now he has shown a regrettable
lack of artistic balance. Nothing that he
does now is pure gold throughout ; one listens

to the finer pages in all his later music as the labourer's son in "Marius the Epicurean" watched his father at work at the brick-kiln— "with a sorrowful distaste for the din and dirt." His new opera, which is to be produced early next year, will probably show whether he is going to realize our best hopes or our worst fears.

COMPOSITIONS OF RICHARD STRAUSS *

Opus 1.† Festival March for Orchestra, 1871.

„ 2. Quartet in A major for 2 Violins, Viola, and Violoncello, 1881.

„ 3.‡ Five Pieces for Pianoforte, 1881.

„ 5. Sonata in B minor for Pianoforte, 1881.

„ 6. Sonata in F major for Violoncello and Piano, 1882–3.

„ 7. Serenade in E flat for Wind Instruments, 1882–3.

„ 8. Concerto in D minor for Violin and Orchestra, 1882–3.

„ 9. Stimmungsbilder for Pianoforte, 1882–3 :
   1. Auf stillem Waldespfad.
   2. An einsamer Quelle.
   3. Intermezzo.
   4. Träumerei.
   5. Haidebild.

„ 10. Eight songs, 1882–3 :
   1. Zueignung.
   2. Nichts.

* London agents: Messrs. Breitkopf Haerkel, 54, Great Mar'borough Street, London, W.

† Opus 1, No. 2, is a song "Einkehr" (1871), the poem by Uhland. It was published in the Strauss number of "Die Musik" (January, 1905). The same poem has been set by Strauss as opus 47, No. 4.

‡ Opus 4 is a Concert Overture, in C minor, that has not yet been published.

3. Die Nacht.
4. Die Georgine.
5. Geduld.
6. Die Verschwiegene.
7. Die Zeitlose.
8. Allerseelen.

Opus 11. Concerto in E flat for French Horn and Orchestra (or Piano), 1883-4.

„ 12. Symphony in F minor for Large Orchestra, 1883-4.

„ 13. Quartet in C minor for Pianoforte, Violin, Viola, and Violoncello, 1883-4.

„ 14. *Wandrers Sturmlied*, for six-part Chorus and Large Orchestra, 1884-5.

„ 15. Five Songs :
1. Madrigal.
2. Winternacht.
3. Lob des Leidens.
4. Aus den Liedern der Trauer.
5. Heimkehr.

„ 16. *Aus Italien :* Symphonic Fantasia for Large Orchestra, 1886.

„ 17. Six Songs :
1. Seitdem dein Aug'.
2. Ständchen.
3. Geheimnis.
4. Vom dunklen Schleier.
5. Nur Mut.
6. Barcarole.

„ 18. Sonata in E flat major, for Violin and Piano, 1887.

Opus 19. *Lotosblätter :* Six Songs, 1887 :
    1. Wozu noch Mädchen.
    2. Breit über mein Haupt.
    3. Schön sind.
    4. Wie sollten wir geheim.
    5. Hoffen.
    6. Mein Herz ist stumm.
„ 20. *Don Juan :* Tone poem (after Lenau)
    for Large Orchestra, 1888.
„ 21. *Schlichte Weisen :* Five Songs, 1888 :
    1. All mein Gedanken.
    2. Du meines Herzens.
    3. Ach Lieb.
    4. Ach weh mir.
    5. Die Frauen sind fromm.
„ 22. *Mädchenblumen :* Four Songs, 1886-7 :
    1. Kornblumen.
    2. Mohnblumen.
    3. Epheu.
    4. Wasserrose.   [1886–7.
„ 23. *Macbeth :* Tone poem for Large Orchestra,
„ 24. *Tod und Verklärung :* Tone poem for
    Large Orchestra, 1889.
„ 25. *Guntram :* Opera in three Acts, 1892–3.
„ 26. Two Songs, 1892–3 :
    1. Frühlingsgedränge.
    2. O wärst du mein.
„ 27. Four Songs, 1892–3 :
    1. Ruhe, mein Seele.
    2. Cäcilie.
    3. Heimliche Aufförderung.
    4. Morgen.

Opus 28. *Till Eulenspiegels lustige Streiche,* for
Large Orchestra, 1894–5.

„ 29. Three Songs, 1894–5 :
1. Traum durch die Dämmerung.
2. Schlagende Herzen.
3. Nachtgang.

„ 30. *Also sprach Zarathustra :* Tone poem for
Large Orchestra, 1894–5.

„ 31. Four Songs, 1896–7 :
1. Blauer Sommer.
2. Wenn!
3. Weisser Jasmin.
4. Stiller Gang.

„ 32. Five Songs, 1896–7 :
1. Ich trage meine Minne.
2. Sehnsucht.
3. Liebeshymnus.
4. O süsser Mai.
5. Himmelsboten.

„ 33. Four Songs with orchestral accompaniment, 1897 :
1. Verführung.
2. Gesang der Apollopriesterin.
3. Hymnus.
4. Pilgers Morgenlied.

„ 34. Two Anthems, for 16-part mixed chorus :
1. Der Abend.
2. Hymne.

„ 35. *Don Quixote.* Fantastic Variations on a
Chevaleresque Theme, for Large Orchestra, 1897.

Opus 36. Four Songs, 1897–8 :
    1. Das Rosenband.
    2. Für 15 Pfennig.
    3. Hat gesagt.
    4. Anbetung.

„ 37. Six Songs, 1897–8 :
    1. Glückes genug.
    2. Ich liebe dich.
    3. Meinem Kinde.
    4. Mein Auge.
    5. Herr Lenz.
    6. Hochzeitslied.

„ 38. Tennyson's "Enoch Arden," Melodrama
    for Voice and Pianoforte, 1897–8.

„ 39. Five Songs, 1897–8 :
    1. Leises Lied.
    2. Jung Hexenlied.
    3. Der Arbeitsmann.
    4. Befreit.
    5. Lied an meinen Sohn.

„ 40. *Ein Heldenleben :* Tone poem for Large
    Orchestra, 1898.

„ 41. Five Songs, 1899–1900 :
    1. Wiegenlied.
    2. In der Campagna.
    3. Am Ufer.
    4. Bruder Liederlich.
    5. Leise Lieder.

„ 42. Two Male-voice Choruses, 1899–1900 :
    1. Liebe.
    2. Altdeutschen Schlachtlied.

Opus 43. Three Songs, 1899–1900 :
1. An Sie.
2. Muttertändelei.
3. Die Ulme zu Hirsau.

„ 44. Two Songs, with orchestral accompaniment, 1899–1900 :
1. Notturno.
2. Nächtlicher Gang.

„ 45. Three Choruses for Male Voices :
1. Schlachtgesang.
2. Lied der Freundschaft.
3. Der Brauttanz.

„ 46. Five Songs, 1899–1900 :
1. Ein Obdach gegen Sturm.
2. Gestern war ich Atlas.
3. Die sieben Siegel.
4. Morgenrot.
5. Ich sehe wie in einen Spiegel.

„ 47. Five Songs, 1899–1900 :
1. Auf ein Kind.
2. Des Dichters Abendgang.
3. Rückleben.
4. Einkehr.
5. Von den sieben Zechbrüdern.

„ 48. Five Songs, 1901 :
1. Freundliche Vision.
2. Ich schwebe.
3. Kling.
4. Winterweihe.
5. Winterliebe.

Opus 49. Eight Songs, 1902 :
1. Waldseligkeit.
2. In goldener Fülle.
3. Wiegenliedchen.
4. Das Lied des Steinklopfers.
5. Sie wissen's nicht.
6. Junggesellenschwur.
7. Wer lieben will, muss leiden.
8. Ach was Kummer, Qual und Schmerzen.

„ 50. *Feuersnot :* Opera, 1900–1901.
„ 51. *Das Tal :* Song for Bass Voice, with orchestral accompaniment, 1903.
„ 52. *Taillefer,* 1903.
„ 53. *Symphonia Domestica,* 1903.
„ 54. *Salome :* Opera, 1906.
„ 55. *Bardengesang,* 1906.
„ 56. Six Songs, 1906 :
1. Gefunden.
2. Blindenklage.
3. Im Spätboot.
4. Mit deinen blauen Augen.
5. Frühlingsfeier.
6. Die heiligen drei Könige aus Morgenland.
„ 57. Two Military Marches, 1906.

WORKS WITHOUT OPUS NUMBERS

Burleske for Piano and Orchestra, 1884–5.
Soldatenlied, for Male-voice Chorus, 1900.
Three Marches, 1906–7.